WHAT STUDENT WRITING
TEACHES US

WHAT STUDENT WRITING TEACHES US

FORMATIVE ASSESSMENT IN THE WRITING WORKSHOP

MARK OVERMEYER

FOREWORD BY JEFF ANDERSON

STENHOUSE PUBLISHERS
PORTLAND, MAINE

Stenhouse Publishers

www.stenhouse.com

Credits

Photographs by Dennis Molitor

Pages 31, 35–36: Figure 3.1, writing prompt, and student samples appear courtesy of the Colorado Department of Education, www.cde.state.co.us. Reprinted with permission.

Library of Congress Cataloging-in-Publication Data

Overmeyer, Mark, 1961-

    What student writing teaches us : formative assessment in the writing workshop / Mark Overmeyer ; foreword by Jeff Anderson.

       p. cm.

    Includes bibliographical references.

    ISBN 978-1-57110-713-8 (alk. paper)

    1. English language—Composition and exercises—Study and teaching (Middle school) 2. English language—Composition and exercises—Evaluation. 3. Educational tests and measurements.

    I. Title.

    LB1631.O85 2009

      808'.042076—dc22

                              2009019938

Cover and interior design by Blue Design (www.bluedes.com)

Manufactured in the United States of America on acid-free, recycled paper
15 14 13 12 11 10 09 9 8 7 6 5 4 3 2

Contents

Foreword

Assessment and *data* have become the two most overused words in education. The problem is, that's all they are: words. Words that label but don't have much meaning, for teachers or students. Words that are used to judge, separate, punish, remediate, level, label, and so forth.

Mark Overmeyer is going to change that perspective on assessment and move our thinking, energy, and focus back where it should be—to the present moment, in our classrooms, listening to and watching our students, and teaching. Instead of combing through data, typing up plans we may or may not use, filling out forms, and collecting more and more data, assessment becomes about real, down-to-earth, in-the-classroom life, taking learners from one place to the next and pushing them just beyond their highest level.

Mark invites us into a thoughtful discussion of what it is to assess, as well as to learn and teach, and how all of these concepts intertwine to give *assessment* meaning beyond the word itself. In this book, Mark took me into a multitude of classrooms across his district. In each place, I could see myself reflected on the page as a learner and an educator. On each page, I found myself thinking about how I let my students know where they are and how we will set goals to move to the next place.

I, like Mark, wonder why we are so obsessed with data about the past. Mark points out the insanity of looking at what children did the year before and making judgments about how to teach them the following year based on a one-time test. It takes a lot of time to scour through numbers and strengths and weaknesses, and too often the data-driven obsession seriously interferes with teaching and learning. *What Student Writing Teaches Us* gives us insight into what assessment really means and addresses the importance of self-assessment and student involvement in this process, which is ever evolving and changing to fit students' needs. If you are a teacher concerned with creating effective writers, Mark will show you some concrete ways you can use assessment to do so. Teaching and assessment—true assessment—are inseparable.

The focus of Mark's book is the most important and often least talked about facet of assessment: formative assessment. Formative assessment is, specifically, assessment *for* learning versus assessment *of* learning. Oh, what a difference a preposition makes in our intentions and the way we view the word *assessment*. Formative assessment is teaching—plain and simple—and Mark shows us that as he guides us through thinking about assessment, and what we should value, in new ways that are refreshing and truly *for* learning.

Mark also helps us problem-solve. How many times have you said, "I know my children know such and such, but they just aren't doing it in their writing"? A very different approach is needed when the problem is about application rather than knowledge. As assessing teachers, we have to understand and clarify that before we begin to address our students' specific needs.

If that's not enough, Mark has the guts to deal with the bugaboo of grades—for an entire chapter, in fact. As a staff developer, I probably get asked about grading more than any other subject. I know that, when I was a student, I felt like Mark did when he was in school: "I did not think of grades as something I could control." Many kids in our classrooms today feel this way, and that's scary. How can you improve or engage with writing if you think that you have no power to effect change in your own writing? As Mark points out, the problem is that assessment is too often considered a final judgment, a grade, the evaluation of what has been learned, or the end of the road. Mark gives us some no-nonsense truths that we all need to remember—or perhaps hear for the first time.

Mark gives us a chance to reflect on our beliefs and our actions. Whether he's addressing clear or high expectations, or how much time students require to show us what they know, Mark continually paints a picture of what can happen in classrooms, ever mindful of the need for practical ways to address assessment issues. I was particularly captured by Mark's story of a student who was struggling with a current piece; the student looked back at an older piece in his portfolio and asked, "Did I write that?" He found his confidence again. The old maxim of a good conference being one that you leave wanting to write holds true here. We all need some confidence to face the blank page or a false start. Is our assessment giving students that confidence?

In the end, Mark brings us around to what has always been true about the teaching and assessment of writing. The focus of our assessment—whether before, during, or after the process of writing and intertwined assessment—should always begin with what is *right* with student writing. For me, remembering that is refreshing, like taking a deep breath. I believe that if we can't find something good in a student's piece of writing, we simply are not looking.

Mark is always looking, much to our benefit.

—Jeff Anderson

Acknowledgments

This book is a true collaboration: I spent two years in elementary and middle school classrooms teaching, talking, listening, and, most of all, learning. Bill Varner, my editor at Stenhouse, helped me organize and focus my ideas, and he also convinced me that I should take on this project even though I felt I had so much to learn about assessment and writing. As it turned out, the need to learn helped me because I had to listen so much to other teachers, experts in the field, and especially to students.

Thank you to Pam Widmann and her many sixth and seventh graders at Liberty Middle School for helping me during the early stages of this book. Even though she was teaching nearly 180 students every day, Pam spent hours with me coteaching, discussing ideas, and looking at student work samples. Her generosity, sense of humor, and masterful teaching made this entire project worthwhile; I am a better teacher and writer today because of Pam.

Jan DiSanti and James Shipp at Eastridge Elementary also opened their rooms to me. Their flexibility and willingness to let me come into their classes with very little notice helped me for two years as I wrote and reworked the ideas in the book. I do not know what I would have done without them, and their students pushed my thinking every step of the way as I wrote and revised the manuscript. Jan and James, your students are very lucky to have been in your classrooms for two years, and I count myself the luckiest of all for the opportunity to learn with you.

Kim Gonzales, a former student who is now a teacher, writer, and friend, agreed to read an early version of my manuscript. Her advice and guidance helped me to clarify my ideas when I needed it the most.

Anne Finseth, a third-grade teacher at Dakota Valley Elementary, brought her student Veronica's picture book to a staff development class one night, and I have used this piece ever since as a training tool to help teachers think of what student writing can teach us. Thank you, Anne and Veronica, for all you have taught me!

Other Colorado teachers who helped me by opening their doors include Sharon Miller and Marlene Lerner at Franklin Elementary in Littleton; Jennifer Frank, Melinda Krause, Allison Robertson, Bea Arteaga, Brad Ayres, Cindy Meyers, and Shannon Keefe from Cherry Creek Schools in Aurora; and all of the teachers at Basalt Elementary in the Roaring Fork Valley. Thanks to all of you for your generosity.

Thanks to fellow Stenhouse writer Jeff Anderson, who provided much-needed encouragement when I had to just press on and finish. Jeff's wonderful books *Mechanically Inclined* and *Everyday Editing* are a constant inspiration as I seek to understand more about how to teach grammar in context. Independent bookseller Sue Lubeck, owner of The Bookies bookstore in Denver, Colorado, asked me about my progress every single time I visited her store, which is often. Thanks, Sue, for always believing I had another book to write, and thanks to Shelly and the rest of the staff at Bookies for helping teachers and children to find just the books they need.

Thank you to my mother, Elaine, and my brother, Scott, who consistently asked how things were going and shared encouraging words. Finally, thank you to Dennis, who lived patiently through this experience of writing a second book.

Introduction

Imagine you are playing the game *Taboo*, and you receive a card with the word *assessment* on the top. Your job is to try to get your team to say the word, with the caveat that you cannot use any of the words listed below the target word. And let's imagine that the forbidden words listed below *assessment* include *grade*, *evaluate*, and *test*. What might you say? What words come to mind?

If you are a teacher, you might think of *rubrics*, but your nonteaching friends might not know this word, and it also seems a bit pretentious, don't you think? And if you are an English teacher, there is always the word *papers*, as in the papers you have to read, those papers that are sitting on your living room table at home. Or maybe they never made their way out of your briefcase. Either way, this game of cards with the word *assessment* on the top will probably cause you to wonder why you are wasting your time with friends playing a silly word game when you should be home grading papers.

In this book, I will share ideas about how teachers and students can use assessment effectively in all stages of the writing process. If our aim is to grow as teachers of writing, and if we want our students to grow as writers, we must not automatically associate assessment with grades and the paper load. Just as we should read student work for reasons other than to grade, students should not always wait for our evaluation to determine their successes and needs as writers. If we do not move from the way many of us were taught—a paper is assigned, and then it is graded—we cannot help our students grow as writers because we are taking out the opportunity to learn through practice. Imagine what would happen if the coach of any sport "graded" every move the team made, or if a piano teacher handed out percentage scores based on how well a student played the piano every time hands were put to keys.

So how do we move from trying to evaluate every piece of writing to using writing as a basis for our teaching? We begin by thinking about the different purposes for assessment. Most of this book will focus on how to use *formative assessment* effectively in the writing classroom. Chapter 1 provides an overview of formative and summative assessment in the context of writing instruction. Chapter 2 discusses how to set the stage for successful writing through meaningful planning. Chapter 3 examines how we can offer feedback through various formats: rubrics, checklists, conferences, and classroom discussions. Chapter 4 brings in the student aspect: How can students effectively monitor their own progress and set goals in order to grow as writers? Finally, in Chapters 5 and 6, we will look at grading practices and record-keeping in the writing workshop.

I do not claim to be an expert in the area of assessment. I am not a statistician, and in the district meetings I frequently attend about data, I am often the one who keeps asking the same questions year after year about what student assessment data actually means for teachers. I am also skeptical about grades, and even as a teacher of graduate students at the University of Colorado at Denver, I worry that my actions do not match my beliefs when I assign point totals and grades to written assignments completed by teachers pursuing their degrees. But being ambivalent about something doesn't make it go away. I had to assign letter grades in writing for fifteen years while teaching grades four through eight, and I continue to assign letter grades to adults. But I must not associate every opportunity to read student work as only a chance to *grade*. My hope is that by thinking deeply about the power of assessment used correctly, we can approach that Sunday night stack of papers with energy, with integrity, and with some new ideas about why and how we assess student writing.

1

Defining Assessment in the Writing Workshop

In the late 1980s, I studied modern dance at the Martha Graham School of Contemporary Dance in New York City. I had been teaching for three years, and I felt it was time to learn something new—not new teaching techniques, but something completely different in a brand-new environment. I purposely set out to learn something that would make me struggle. Though I was interested in dance, I had never taken classes until that year. A phone call to the Martha Graham School confirmed that they took beginners: I was assured there were no prerequisites. I spent six memorable weeks in the back of the dance studio, trying to hide behind twenty-five people younger and shorter than me, desperate to blend in even though I am 6′ 4″. I towered over everyone as I sought to learn the meaning of *struggle*.

And struggle I did. But I also learned about myself and about teaching. When I look back on my experiences at the dance studio, I admire my teachers for allowing me to stay. I was so clearly out of my league. Each day, my teachers explained and modeled each move in great detail. Even though I rarely, if ever, produced a move that resembled what the teacher wanted, it was *clear* what was expected, and the teacher taught me to *practice* meaningfully so that I did improve. The standards were high, and they were never lowered for my benefit. I never reached the level of the other students—I remained a beginner for the entire six weeks—but I did make noticeable improvement, and I did make progress toward their very clear standards. I was never sent to a corner of the room to try out easier dance moves, nor was I ever told I couldn't try. I have never worked harder, and one day my teacher recognized me for my effort: "Many of you have talent in this room. But no one works harder than Mark." I have never been prouder.

Modeling, clear expectations, and meaningful practice toward a standard: these elements helped me to get better even though I knew I would never trade my teaching credentials for a career in dance. I began to see how the teaching techniques in the arts, much like the techniques of coaches in various sports, differ from typical classroom teaching, mainly because of how assessment is used. The teachers at the Martha Graham School engaged in effective assessment practices, whether they knew it or not, because they consistently clarified key learning targets, scaffolded support to meet the needs of each student, and monitored each student's growth. After the first few painful classes, I emerged from the studio each day a bit less sore and a bit more confident. I could feel my body slowly becoming more limber, and after a couple of weeks, I knew when I was not completing a move correctly even though it was nearly impossible for me to actually complete the move. In other words, I was self-assessing, and by the end of the summer I began to correct my own mistakes as I relied less and less on teacher feedback. Had the Graham School only been involved in "grading" or evaluating my actual performance, I certainly would not have received a passing grade. Yet I grew because I was in an environment rich with formative assessment.

Defining Formative Assessment

High-stakes standardized testing captures so much attention in the media and in our schools that we often associate assessment with a final grade or score. In Colorado, for example, the state test, given in the spring in grades three through ten, provides the only student performance data that is used to grade each school in our state. In such a system, it is hard to remember that assessment means so much more than a test score. We should use assessment data to learn how to grow, but since we don't even get our scores back until the following school year and we are never allowed to view the actual tests after students complete them, it is difficult to use our state test to meaningfully guide our instruction.

When many of us think back to our own experiences with assessment in English classes, our memories are probably full of "assign and grade" examples. We were assigned work, the teacher graded it, and we moved on to the next assignment. We did not learn from the letter grade at the top of the paper, even if it was good. I remember many times when I felt relieved to receive an A or a B, but I never remember feeling confidence as a writer if I did receive a high mark. If I received less than a B, I was disappointed, but I attributed this disappointment to some random method the teacher used to score my work: I did not think of grades as something I could control. High-stakes testing might be likened to this "assign and grade" mentality, just on a larger scale. Schools are "assigned" to administer the tests and then receive "grades" based on an average of all students' scores.

Final grades on papers and high-stakes testing showcase assessment as something that happens only at the end of an assignment or a course—summative assessment. But assessment can and should be so much more. As teachers of writing, we can monitor student progress during all parts of the writing process, even during the initial, idea-gathering stages, by thinking of assessment as something that can inform our instruction—formative, rather than summative, assessment. In fact, if we truly want to use assessment to guide our instruction, we should not wait until a piece of writing is "finished" in order to determine a logical instructional move. If our goal as writing teachers is to help our students improve, then waiting until the end is too late—in fact, "the end" should only happen when students literally leave our classrooms because of semester or year-end breaks.

Black, Harrison, Lee, Marshall, and Wiliam clarify the difference between formative and summative assessment in their article "Working Inside the Black Box" (2004):

> *Assessment for learning is any assessment for which the first priority in its design and practice is to serve the purpose of promoting students' learning. It thus differs from assessment designed primarily to serve the purposes of accountability, or of ranking, or of certifying competences. An assessment activity can help learning if it provides information that teachers and their students can use as feedback in assessing themselves and one another and in modifying the teaching and learning activities in which they are engaged. Such assessment becomes "formative assessment" when the evidence is actually used to adapt the teaching work to meet learning needs. (10; emphasis mine)*

In order to adapt our teaching to meet students' needs, we must consider how to effectively implement formative assessment, or assessment *for learning*. Summative assessment, as described in the article, is assessment *of learning*, which often leads to class ranks and a final score, and therefore provides limited opportunity for students to grow.

James Popham, the author of *Transformative Assessment*, brings students into the picture with his definition of formative assessment: "Formative assessment is a planned process in which teachers or students use assessment-based evidence to adjust what they are currently doing" (2008, 6). When a Title I reading teacher plans lessons *before* teaching to meet the needs of the students he greets every morning, he is using formative assessment. When a science teacher notices that students are ready to move more quickly through material *while she is teaching* and then increases the pace accordingly, she is involved in formative assessment. When a student is very clear about expectations for reaching a standard in an English classroom and adjusts his writing *after leaving class that day* to meet this standard, he is monitoring his own learning, and is therefore engaged in formative assessment.

When we break Popham's definition apart a bit, we find some ways teachers can use the ideas of formative assessment to inform their teaching practices.

A key word in Popham's formative assessment definition is *planned*. While formative assessment may seem to encourage teaching "on the fly," what it really requires is clear expectations about what we want students to know and be able to do, and knowledge of strategies that will allow students to achieve these learning outcomes. Chapter 2 will provide more examples of how to plan effectively in the writing classroom so that formative assessment practices can be put to their best use.

Popham's formative assessment definition asks teachers and students to "use assessment-based evidence," and in the writing classroom this translates into feedback. One way the Graham School helped me to improve was the immediacy and clarity of the feedback provided. Teachers watched my performance every day, and they provided me with something specific to work on. They chose these goals carefully because they knew I could only handle small steps, and each goal was based on their high standards. Chapter 3 will examine feedback in the writing workshop through the lens of rubrics, conferences, and classroom discussions.

One of my favorite words in Popham's formative assessment definition is *students*. Students must be involved in the assessment of their writing. While visiting classrooms in preparation for writing this book, I was impressed with how much our students can tell us about their own needs as learners. Throughout this book, you will read stories of kindergartners clearly describing their writing processes, in addition to excerpts from a middle school class discussion about the most effective settings for writing practice.

When we include students in our thinking about assessment, we are accomplishing so much. We are lifting the burden of "grading," because if we are used to thinking of assessment *only* as grading, the mere inclusion of students in the process will surely make us think of assessment a little bit differently. We are also erasing the burden of being the expert in the room with all the answers. Natalie Goldberg, one of my favorite authors who gives advice to writers, ends one of her essays this way: "Finally, don't listen to me. What do I know? Go out there yourself into the open page" (1991, 9).

Goldberg's statement appears to contradict the idea that we can advise our student writers, but I think she is encouraging writers to rely on themselves after they think about the advice they have been given. In classroom settings, I believe we will become more effective teachers when we encourage students to become aware of their own strengths and needs. In the context of teaching writing, especially in the field of assessment, we have too often left our students out of the picture. Student-friendly rubrics and criteria lists, discussed in Chapter 3 of this book, have helped to bring students into the discussion, but what Goldberg and Popham are charging us with as teachers of writing takes this idea of students' being involved in their own learning one giant step further. They are reminding us that we as writing teachers cannot be the ones who know everything. We must let go.

Chapter 4 provides more ideas for involving students in the assessment process, and Chapter 5 focuses on evaluation and grading practices. Finally, in Chapter 6, I discuss record-keeping and suggest how we might read student writing for various purposes.

I feel like I embody Natalie Goldberg's statement much of the time when I think about assessment. After all, what *do* I know? What can I offer to this field of assessment? When I think of myself as a learner rather than an expert, however, I hope I can offer some guidance. When I look back on my six-week intensive course at the Graham School, I realize in retrospect that the entire point was to *learn*, not to become an expert. I came to understand more about myself as a learner during that six-week stint than in my entire academic career. The opportunity to think about assessment for the past two years as I prepared to write this book has left me in the same position: I have learned so much, and though I still have many questions, my new learning has left me with strongly held beliefs.

Assessment, when used correctly in a formative way, can empower students and teachers not only to improve but, better yet, to *believe* in themselves as writers and teachers of writing. And once students believe they *are* writers and you believe you *are* a teacher of writing, any barrier, no matter how imposing, begins to crumble.

2

2

Formative Assessment in Action: Setting the Stage for Success

For many years, I began my day with sentence-correcting exercises for my intermediate and middle school students. I would write a sentence with several errors on the board, and they corrected these sentences while I gathered homework, took lunch count, and generally prepared for the day.

My students were normally quiet during these exercises, which at that time made me think they were actually learning. Looking back, I realize they were not actually learning much; they were just being compliant. But one memorable day, a noncompliant voice finally made me think about what I was doing as a teacher: when Jonathan saw the sentence on the board—something full of errors like, "Me and jane goed to the store last wendesday"—he blurted out, "Why are we doing this? No one makes that many mistakes!"

I include this story in a book about assessment because I believe that if we know our students and plan to meet their needs, and if we read their writing because we want to *learn* and not just *grade*, we can become more effective teachers. My students were not benefiting from day-starter grammar exercises, and even though I knew they were not transferring the skills they practiced each day to their own writing, I did not change my practice because I had a teacher's guide that tempted me to automatically turn to the next exercise. I was not effectively planning for instruction because I just kept turning pages, and therefore I provided no opportunities for formative assessment.

Luckily, Jonathan stopped me dead in my tracks and made me think about what I was doing. From that day forward, I planned differently: I often started the day with a writing exercise that required students to produce something they wanted to share, and if I used a correction exercise, I connected the exercise to something I noticed in their writing. In other words, I focused my instruction by assessing my students' needs—not *grading*, but *assessing*. And one of the most effective ways to assess needs is to plan effectively up front to make sure that meaningful assessment, and therefore meaningful practice, can occur.

Using Standards to Set the Stage

If I want to set up my classroom so I can provide the most effective, meaningful assessment, where do I begin? The cardinal rule of teaching is to know your students, and I agree completely with this. In the context of writing instruction, this has been translated into the idea of teaching the writer, not the writing. This chapter will address some ideas for planning according to standards, including thoughts about how to meet the needs of the students in front of you.

So which standards should we consult as we think about writing? I believe that standards are helpful in planning for instruction as long as they are full of rich opportunity for thinking about our writing.

Though specific writing standards vary from state to state, the standards published by the National Council of Teachers of English (NCTE) and the

International Reading Association (IRA) in 1996 provide helpful frameworks for all teachers. As stated in the first chapter of the NCTE/IRA standards document, the purpose of the standards is to prepare students for the future, to develop a shared vision of expectations among all stakeholders (teachers, researchers, parents, etc.), and to promote high educational expectations (1996). Because these standards address helping students to use effective writing processes, they are not reductive and can be effective tools for planning.

The standards specific to writing include the following:

- Standard 4: Students adjust their use of spoken, written, and visual language to communicate effectively with a variety of audiences and for different purposes. (33)
- Standard 5: Students employ a wide variety of strategies as they write and use different writing process elements appropriately to communicate with different audiences for a variety of purposes. (35)
- Standard 6: Students apply knowledge of language structure, language conventions, media techniques, figurative language, and genre to create, critique, and discuss print and nonprint texts. (36)

A powerful statement about goals appears in the explanation of Standard 5:

Students who write in the context of meaningful goals are more likely to work carefully to shape and revise what they compose. Teachers can create a sense of the purposefulness of writing by helping students to consider the needs of their audiences as they compose, edit, and revise. (NCTE/IRA 1996, 36)

The creators of this standards document are stating something I have believed for a long time: If students have a compelling reason to write, then they tend to write more effectively. But if the bulk of the reasons they write are "just for school," then they begin to limit themselves to a narrow audience (the teacher, and perhaps other students) and a narrow purpose (to get a good enough grade to pass). In the planning stages, then, we should consider our students' needs and their progress toward a standard, and we should always consider why we are asking students to write.

Let's consider an example of how knowledge of standards and students might help us to plan effectively. Jennifer Frank asked me to come to her fourth-grade classroom at Ponderosa Elementary in Aurora, Colorado, to model a lesson on persuasive writing. Many resources came to mind immediately. Gretchen Bernabei and Barry Lane's hilarious book *Why We Must Run with Scissors* (2001) is full of ideas for helping students become more effective persuasive writers, and because Barry Lane knows what appeals to kids, many of his ideas are full of humor. I also frequent the NCTE-sponsored website www.readwritethink.org when I need ideas for teaching, because the site allows me to search for writing ideas that meet specific standards. But even a standards-based, motivating idea may not meet the needs of the specific students I am working with. I knew Jennifer's students had just met their new principal, Mrs. Sloan. I planned my persuasive writing lesson around Standard 5 because it discusses writing for specific audiences and purposes. Keeping the students in mind, I thought about Barry Lane's ideas for motivating students, and I also thought about how these students had just met their new principal.

Since I have worked with intermediate students for many years, I knew going in that when they think of what they might change in school, they often think of more recess. In the planning stages, I came up with a "real" reason to write (more recess), and provided an authentic audience (the new principal). As soon as I explained the idea of writing a letter to Mrs. Sloan to ask for more recess, one girl in the class, DaVida, asked, "Can we give our letters to the principal?"

I said yes, if they thought they were well written and might make a difference, and they seemed motivated to write. A key teaching point in the lesson involved avoiding the use of whining. We talked about how whining might be an effective tool in some contexts (an alarming number of students told me how many times whining worked well when they wanted something from their parents), but that we needed to avoid whining in our letters. Students needed to come up with real, concrete reasons for wanting more recess. DaVida was working within the standard that asks students to consider various audiences and purposes while they write. Even though I had suggested the idea of writing to Mrs. Sloan, I think it was the possibility that the writing might be read and might have an impact that caused some students to write more carefully, and in some cases even passionately. Had I not planned effectively and instead just followed some scripted lesson that dictated exactly how students were to persuade, this moment might not have happened. Keeping our particular students and the standards in mind while we plan is an essential first step to success in the writing workshop.

Planning Ahead for What Might Need to Change

A key component to effective planning is providing opportunities to adjust our instruction to meet the needs of our students. But what do we adjust? For many years, I have gathered ideas from other teachers, resource books, and the Internet. I used to look for the perfect mini-lessons, and I measured the success of the lessons I collected by how engaged my students were. If they liked the lesson, I saved it in a file. If they did not like the lesson, then I tried to change it or I abandoned it. There were a couple of problems with this approach to planning. First, I was not really thinking much about how the lesson might meet the needs of the students in front of me when I pulled out certain "surefire" ideas year after year; I was just remembering how well a lesson had worked before. In other words, I was not basing my instructional plans on an assessment of what my current students needed; I was planning based on how students had responded to the lesson the year before. Second, I was not considering how each lesson might be altered to make a true difference for my current students. Even my standards-based lessons weren't necessarily meeting the needs of the students as much as they were meeting my desire to teach to the standards.

I propose three things we might consider adjusting in the planning stages of our writing instruction in order to meet our students' needs: time, topic choice, and talk.

Time

We all feel the pressure of time in our teaching lives. We just don't have enough time, and if students were just with us longer, we could make an impact. We worry about having enough time every day, and then we wonder if the time we do spend provides enough opportunities for students to grow as writers.

The first questions we should ask ourselves as teachers of writing deal with time. One important question is, How much time do I set aside for my students to meaningfully write each day? Writing here is defined as composing; spelling, handwriting exercises, vocabulary, and grammar exercises taught out of context are not included. The key to time is how meaningful it is: when students are creating their own writing, they are learning.

When we consider time a bit differently in the context of assessment, we link time spent writing to achievement. We might ask: How can we adjust the use of time we have during a writing workshop to best support student achievement? Is the traditional structure of a five- to ten-minute mini-lesson, an extended thirty- to forty-minute writing time, and a ten-minute sharing time the best way to help all students improve? While this structure does work for many students, especially when they are engaged in authentic purposes for writing, I believe, after observing hundreds of students write over the years, that the writing time in the workshop might need to be a bit more flexible. More time may help some students to improve, but it is also possible that less time will help others.

There are many ways we can help our students feel successful in short periods of time. For example, we can use quick writes—timed, free-choice, or prompted writings—to practice fluency. Donald Graves and Penny Kittle's book *Inside Writing* (2005) provides many examples of how quick-write exercises can be used to increase student confidence in writing. In a writing workshop I attended, poet Lisa Zimmerman referred to the quick writes we wrote as "prompts," and the teacher hackles in me went up a bit because of testing. I hear "prompt" and I think "random, required writing topic I know nothing about that will be graded." But when I asked Zimmerman about her use of the word "prompts," she said: "I think of a prompt as a ramp to thinking. The prompt helps you to get words on the page."

Quick-write exercises allow students to practice writing in a nonthreatening, short time frame. They are like ramps, to use Zimmerman's term, for getting ready for the work to come. Many students (and adults) who do not care to write feel some success with these quick writes. If the routine of thirty- to forty-minute writing blocks every day is not supporting student achievement, then one way to alter our instruction is to give *less* time rather than *more*. This may seem counterintuitive, possibly even "anti-workshop," but let me share an example.

One of my favorite books is Cynthia Rylant's *In November* (2000). I have often used this book as a mentor text for descriptive writing. Many students are impressed with how perfectly Rylant captures the fall and the Thanksgiving holiday in so few words. Her book is a perfect example of showing rather than telling—writing that shows us precisely what is happening using sensory details.

I often encourage students to try creating seasonal writing based on the craft in Rylant's text. Josh, a fifth-grade student in my class one year, created his own "In November" piece after listening to and discussing Rylant's text:

> In November the air is dense with smog from the fireplace. To people's relief, November accepts the heavy snow. People dream of Thanksgiving and the massive feast. You can hear the shouts of happy kids and laughter echo through the air. From inside you can hear them stomp through the snow and bombard each other with snowballs. Plus you can smell the delicious Thanksgiving feast cooking on the stove. In November you can feel the icy snow climb into your boots. Also you can hear the "slush" of cars speeding through the snow. Plus you can feel the icy, cold, barren air numb out your cheeks. November is a month unlike any other.

Josh did not spend more than ten minutes on this piece, he did no revisions, and he was very proud of the result.

Later in the year, when Josh was struggling to complete a four-week unit on research-based writing, I pulled his November writing from his folder to boost his confidence—and when he read it, he asked, "Did I write this?"

When I think of this story now in the context of time and assessment, I realize that one of the issues for Josh was time—not too little, but too much. He saw his four-week research project as cumbersome. Josh was using his forty-minute blocks of writing each day, but I realized too late in the process that he was abandoning his ideas several times during each writing block. He would write for a few minutes, and then either erase, cross out, or throw away his paper. Extended time for writing for self-selected purposes was not the answer for Josh. Now, I would go back and restructure the workshop time into "November-sized" chunks, asking Josh to create short sections of the final project each day, bit by bit, and then put all the pieces together at the end. In other words, we would work to make sure that the time he had was well used—I waited too long to prevent his frustration with writing.

While I believe the primary purpose of quick writes is to improve fluency, encourage idea generation, and boost confidence, I think we can also use quick writes as evidence of student success. The short piece Josh created about November proved he met the standard about using effective word choice. He knew how to create pictures in a reader's mind. So even though he did not revise, edit, or publish this piece, and I did not grade it or score it on a rubric because the intent was to practice a craft technique, I know this piece meets the standard for writing in the descriptive mode. Do I want struggling writers like Josh to feel success in longer, published pieces? Of course. But I am not going to dismiss a piece of data about writing just because it came from a practice exercise that took very little time. This is one of those situations when we need to think of what we mean by "assess"—and here, I mean that I can read any piece of writing to notice how a student is progressing toward meeting a standard.

Topic Choice

When we consider how to help our students become better writers, choice is a common consideration. How much choice do we give our students, and if they had more choices, would they be better writers? When planning for instruction, we choose texts for writing models, and we also consider choices students will have as writers in the workshop. As we think about choice as it relates to assessment, I want to think about both ends of the spectrum: from free choice to limited choices.

One of my favorite stories about teaching comes from my experiences with Jim, a fifth-grade student. He did not like to write or read—or, to be fair, he did not like to write or read what I wanted him to write and read about. He was not enthusiastic about Cynthia Rylant, Patricia Polacco, Jane Yolen, and other descriptive writers I shared with the class that year. He was not particularly excited when I read *In November*, though he dutifully wrote descriptive pieces about seasons. Jim was willing to write and read, but even when he had many choices for his reading material, I often required everyone to be part of a novel group. He didn't care much for novels.

What Jim liked was cars. He read *Car and Driver*, and yes, I admit I confiscated a few of his magazines on more than one occasion and asked him to pick them up at the end of the day because they prevented him from focusing on what *I* deemed was important. Jim not only liked cars, he knew about cars. I wish now I could go back in time and change my plans to allow Jim to show his progress in writing by producing pieces about cars. I finally did allow this beginning in about April, but I wasted a lot of time up until then. It wasn't so much that I told Jim not to write about cars, but I wasn't providing models of writing that gave him "permission" to write about cars. The texts I chose appealed to *me,* and I assumed they appealed to my students as well. My breakthrough came one day while we were studying advice columns in a mini-lesson. I gave Jim a clipboard and paper and told him to write down the names of all the cars in the parking lot, research who the cars belonged to, and then offer advice about new cars for the staff. Because the topic appealed to him so much, Jim loved creating this list, though he was appalled when he found out that my car was the "most uncool" car in the lot.

What I learned from Jim is that, sometimes, choice is what it takes. I say "sometimes" because I also believe that limited choices help some writers. I visited Shannon Keefe's second-grade classroom at Polton Elementary in Aurora, Colorado, one day while her students were writing or sharing ideas quietly with a partner. When I asked one student what she was writing about, she said: "I'm writing a story about being locked out of my house, and my baby brother is inside. I have to figure out how to get back in before my parents get home." I thought this was a great story idea. I asked another student about his writing, and he said: "I'm pretending I have a baby brother and he's locked in the house and I am trying to figure out how to get back in."

I realized the students were writing to a prompt—a story idea the teacher had given them all to write about. Many of us who feel well versed in the writing workshop would feel this is limiting, but to that I would say it is much more complicated than you might think. Shannon's students were all engaged. Some of them sustained their writing time for nearly forty minutes that day, and Shannon told me many continued their stories during the rest of the week. But here is what Shannon's students taught me that day about choice, and why I mention *less* choice as a possibility for getting the best writing out of students: all of the writing was interesting. Each student had a different way of trying to get in the house, and they each developed a level of specific details that made every story completely different from the others. If Shannon was assessing her students' ability to create stories with strong leads, specific details, and sequenced events, they all would have met those standards. The best part was the excitement in the room. Shannon shared with me later that some of her students had not written much at all before, and that this prompted writing exercise provided a kind of breakthrough. When I asked Shannon's students what they thought of their stories, they were universally positive.

Shannon planned with standards in mind, and when she came across a "canned" prompt idea in a resource book, she believed the story-starter would motivate her students, so she used it. Shannon would have allowed students to choose another idea for a story if they had asked, but in this case, they didn't. I would consider the prompt Shannon gave her students a "framed" choice. In other words, there were many possibilities within the story idea she presented, but the few details she provided were interesting enough for everyone to get excited about writing. To be honest, if I was in her class, I, too, would have enjoyed writing a story about being locked out of the house with a little brother left inside. Based on what Shannon told me about her students, wide-open choice would not have resulted in such well-written stories from all of her students. Her assessment of their progress was actually made more accurate because she limited the choices instead of broadening them. The moral of the story is that when it comes to choice, we might assume that more choice is better, but we might also consider less choice if we want to see what our students can do.

Talk

I am always impressed with how effectively even young students can verbalize their thinking when a teacher encourages and expects meaningful talk. At all levels, from kindergarten to high school, it is such a joy to visit these literate environments. First graders in particular have convinced me that we don't have to worry so much about knowing everything and controlling every moment. When first graders have an idea, they just pipe up and say it—all we have to do is provide the opportunities for talk.

I asked a group of first graders at Basalt Elementary in Basalt, Colorado, to tell me if I was reading the Cynthia Rylant book *Night in the Country* (1991) correctly. I encouraged them to tell me if they thought I could do a better job. I opened to the first page of this very descriptive illustrated book, ignored the real words on the page, and said, "I see owls." Then I turned to a page with an illustration of a frog and said, "I hear frogs." One girl interrupted my "reading" and said, "That's wrong!"

"How do you know?" I asked. "My words match the pictures on the page. How do you know that what I said is not what Cynthia Rylant wrote?"

"Because who would buy a book like that?" she asked.

Who indeed. And a six-year-old just demonstrated that she knows that writers can use language to delight, not just to inform. I didn't have to give a test or plan an expansive lesson for this student to show me what she knew. If we provide moments for talk and chart what students are learning, we can build a list of tools students can use in their writing.

Sharon Miller's second graders at Franklin Elementary in Littleton, Colorado, were getting ready for writer's workshop one day. I noticed chart paper in front of the room titled "Writer's Tools," and below it, a bulleted list contained items like these: *strong leads*, *words that make pictures for the reader*, *active verbs*, and *similes and metaphors*. When I asked Sharon's students about the list, they were proud to tell me they created it while noticing things about texts that they read or their teacher read to them.

During writer's workshop, Sharon's students talk a lot. I first learned about the power of talk in the writing classroom from Katie Wood Ray. Her books *Wondrous Words* (1999), *About the Authors* (2004), and *Study Driven* (2007) are full of descriptions of how teachers can invite students to discuss mentor texts. For the purposes of this book, I want to frame this idea of talk in terms of how it can be used as a formative assessment tool in the writing classroom.

When I think of Sharon Miller's classroom in terms of assessment, it is important to know a few things first. Sharon did not ask only the most advanced writers to engage in talk about writing. Sharon's students are just like the rest of us: some walk in the door full of ideas for writing workshop, while others seem to spend half the period of the first workshop trying to find a pencil. Sharon read aloud books to her students that were often beyond their independent reading level—she chose rich texts to read aloud and study because she knew her students needed rich texts in order to notice writing craft. She differentiated by reading these books aloud, and then she followed up by also asking students to notice craft techniques in the books they were reading independently.

Sharon asked all students to talk with her and with each other about what they noticed, and this is where her formative assessment really began. She not only asked them to talk—she expected them to. She helped them form complete sentences while they shared their ideas out loud. Remember that formative assessment is a *planned* process, and Sharon intentionally planned in advance to provide opportunities for all students to access strong mentor texts and to be engaged in meaningful talk about writing.

In addition to modeling how to form complete thoughts and complete sentences about craft techniques, Sharon built in time for her students to find writing partners to practice talking in pairs. She knew her students needed to be independent enough to share their ideas with each other; once she was confident they had the knowledge of writing craft techniques necessary to engage in a conversation, she modeled how these partnered dialogues should sound. Students practiced taking turns, responding to their partners, and offering suggestions. Because of her careful planning, when I asked Sharon's students about writing, they literally knew what they were talking about.

Across the hall from Sharon, second-grade teacher Marlene Lerner also planned classroom discussions about what writers do. I visited her classroom after she had focused her writing lessons on the importance of specific details. Specificity is something I love to teach students about because I find most students can easily find success by being more specific. Instead of writing "my brother," for example, writing "Scott" or "my older brother, Scott" is better— just adding a name can make writing more interesting.

Marlene told me before I visited the class that one of her students, Jackson, had some ideas of his own about being specific. And sure enough, when I walked in the room, he asked if he could talk to me.

"I want to talk to you about being specific," he said.

"You must be Jackson! Your teacher told me you had some ideas about specific versus general writing," I said, after introducing myself.

"I think if you are too specific, it gets boring. Sometimes it's better to be general."

It was clear to me that Jackson had, indeed, put a lot of thought into his ideas.

"So you mean that sometimes you shouldn't be too specific?" I asked.

"Yes. Sometimes it is better to be general."

"So if I ask you what you had for dinner last night, it's better if you say 'Pizza' than if you say, 'I had spicy pepperoni and sausage—'"

Jackson cut me off: "Right—you wouldn't say, 'I had hot pepperoni pizza with a chewy, delicious crust.' No one talks like that." He picked up a book on his desk. "If every page of this book had specific details like that, it'd be boring."

I was just about to say something about how talking is different from writing when he said, "But if a book is too general, it's boring too."

"So what should we do when we write? Should we be specific or general?"

"I think we need a balance," Jackson said. "We need some specific details, and some general."

Jackson's "just-right" theory of writing is not only perceptive in its own right, but my exchange with him confirms my belief that so much of what we need to learn about teaching is right in front of us. We just need to ask the right questions of our students and then listen to what they have to say. When we listen carefully, we can assess what they know and what they need. Jackson knew that statements such as "specific writing is good writing" do not always hold true, and he wanted to share this. He needed the opportunity to be heard, and because his teacher listens to her students, he knew he belonged in the community of writers. Jackson was part of an ongoing classroom discussion where all ideas were welcomed, not just those of a teacher, a rubric, or a list of standards. Marlene routinely tweaks the checklists her students use as they uncover truths together about how to become better writers. Marlene's students are lucky that she knows this work is a bit messy and perhaps even uncomfortable at times, but as they all work together to understand more about writing and writers, and as they listen to each other, they all benefit and grow.

We can assess students' learning from one-on-one talks like the dialogue I had with Jackson, and we can also use whole-class discussions to guide our teaching. A visit to a fourth-grade classroom provides an example of how talk can be used as a tool for effective planning, and therefore an integral part of formative assessment.

During the first weeks of school in James Shipp's fourth-grade class at Eastridge Elementary in Aurora, Colorado, students had been working on pieces about their futures. They were encouraged to imagine they were famous, and to write pieces that included details about their fame. Many students imagined being sports stars or famous singers, and they described their homes and their lives in great detail. In order to assess what they understood about the qualities of good writing, James asked five students to share their pieces in front of the class. I set a purpose for listening: I asked students to listen for specific details they thought made the shared writing more interesting.

After the first student read, we began to list on the board what we noticed. The first reader used many descriptive adjectives and specific nouns to make her piece come alive. Students identified these words while I listed them on the board. Many people believe that students do not learn grammar in the elementary grades, and this is why they develop "bad habits" as they enter middle and high school. I do not find this to be true at all when students understand the *purpose* of grammar. James's students were able to identify nouns and adjectives because he had taught them how knowledge of these types of words can lead to effective writing products.

After listing words on the board, I asked students to reread their own writing, circle the adjectives and specific nouns they'd used, and add adjectives and specific nouns in their writing where it would result in a stronger piece.

I was trying to assess student understanding of the language of writing prior to reading their pieces myself. If they were unable to identify the qualities they admired in a piece, then I needed to know that prior to reading their work. I would have to spend more time practicing the language of writing craft techniques before asking them to read their own work with these crafts in mind. My ultimate goal is for students to revise their own work. I want students to seek support from me and from peers when they need it, but if they consistently ask me "Is this good?" then I worry they have not internalized the qualities of good writing. By asking them up front what they notice, I can begin to understand what I may still need to teach them.

This type of assessment is formative because I am not evaluating—I am not ending my thinking about what these students know and are able to do. Rather, I am trying to get a general understanding of what they know so that I can tweak the teaching points I have in mind for that day. I am using student talk to make authentic decisions about what to teach, so I am planning for instruction as I learn what students understand.

When students talk about each other's writing, even during early draft stages, teaching points emerge. Several students in James's class did not know similes by name even though they wrote them. Max shared that he would have a carpet "as red as an apple" in his mansion, and students identified this as descriptive writing. I asked them if they knew what writers call phrases such as this that compare, and when no one knew, I told them it was a simile. I then asked if anyone else had used a simile. Several students raised their hands: Jose mentioned that his couch was "soft as if it was filled with water," and another student spoke of silver cars "glittering like diamonds." Students discovered similes in their writing, and we added them to the list of writing tools.

One of the benefits to this inquiry-based approach of asking students what they notice is that the teacher can assess students authentically. I do not need to read through 100 student papers to know if my students understand the importance of adding details. I am asking them to do the assessment work up front by listening to a few pieces shared by their peers, naming what they notice, and then immediately checking their own work for these same types of details. While it is certainly possible that not all students will be able to identify these strong qualities in their own work or make their own work better, I am providing an opportunity early on for students to connect the discussions about good writing to themselves. If students cannot effectively talk about what they notice in writing, I will bring them along by helping them to notice craft elements in others' writing—both professional writing and student writing. This will increase the likelihood that they will produce strong writing on their own.

Planning with Time, Topic Choice, and Talk in Mind

Standard by standard, here is a list of questions that may guide some thinking about how to assess student progress. The three standards listed here, mentioned earlier in the chapter, are from the NCTE/IRA document *Standards for the English Language Arts* (1996). The questions use the frames of reference of time, topic choice, and talk as a way to structure planning. They are included in this chapter about planning because I believe that if we think carefully up front about what we want to do as teachers, then we will be more freed up to alter our instruction if everything does not go exactly according to plan. See Figure 2.1 for an alternative formatting of this information.

Figure 2.1
Planning Table

STANDARD 4: Students adjust their use of spoken, written, and visual language to communicate effectively with a variety of audiences and for different purposes.	**STANDARD 5:** Students employ a wide variety of strategies as they write and use different writing process elements appropriately to communicate with different audiences for a variety of purposes.	**STANDARD 6:** Students apply knowledge of language structure, language conventions, media techniques, figurative language, and genre to create, critique, and discuss print and nonprint texts.
TIME: Have I planned multiple opportunities for students to demonstrate their sense of audience in many time frames? For example, have I planned opportunities for students to develop work over time for a larger audience than the classroom, and have I planned shorter, quick-write opportunities for students to create pieces they might share only with peers?	**TIME:** Have I planned opportunities for students to try out writing strategies in different time frames? For example, have I used quick writes intentionally for descriptive writing or thesis development rather than just asking students to apply these writing strategies over long periods of time?	**TIME:** Have I planned opportunities for students to practice conventions and craft in both short and long periods of time?
TOPIC CHOICE: Have I planned opportunities for students to choose their topics based on their own purposes? For example, if I am asking students to write personal narratives, will I provide choices not only for what they will write a narrative about but also who they are writing it for?	**TOPIC CHOICE:** Have I provided students with a wide range of possibilities for getting work done? Do my students feel comfortable during workshop time, consulting quietly with others, reading, and even drawing in order to get their words on the page? Do they think of writing time as only solitary and silent, or do they see choices appropriate to their own process?	**TOPIC CHOICE:** Have I planned opportunities for students to choose genres appropriate to their purpose and audience?
TALK: Have I planned opportunities for students to talk about their purposes and audiences in the beginning stages of the writing process and as pieces are being created? For example, will I ask students to choose a very particular audience prior to writing and then ask them to discuss this audience with peers before they even get started?	**TALK:** Have I planned opportunities for students to talk about their own writing processes? What might I do to help students feel comfortable enough with their own processes to discuss them with others? Have I scheduled enough time for talk during all parts of the writing process?	**TALK:** Have I planned opportunities for students to talk with others about their understanding of language structure, conventions, and figurative language? Can they serve as peer revision buddies when others in the class need support?

STANDARD 4: Students adjust their use of spoken, written, and visual language to communicate effectively with a variety of audiences and for different purposes.

GUIDING QUESTIONS

- Have I planned multiple opportunities for students to demonstrate their sense of audience in many time frames? For example, have I planned opportunities for students to develop work over time for a larger audience than the classroom, and have I planned shorter, quick-write opportunities for students to create pieces they might share only with peers?

- Have I planned opportunities for students to choose their topics based on their own purposes? For example, if I am asking students to write personal narratives, will I provide choices not only for what they will write a narrative about but also who they are writing it for?

- Have I planned opportunities for students to talk about their purposes and audiences in the beginning stages of the writing process and as pieces are being created? For example, will I ask students to choose a very particular audience prior to writing and then ask them to discuss this audience with peers before they even get started?

STANDARD 5: Students employ a wide variety of strategies as they write and use different writing process elements appropriately to communicate with different audiences for a variety of purposes.

GUIDING QUESTIONS

- Have I planned opportunities for students to try out writing strategies in different time frames? For example, have I used quick writes intentionally for descriptive writing or thesis development rather than just asking students to apply these writing strategies over long periods of time?

- Have I provided students with a wide range of possibilities for getting work done? Do my students feel comfortable during workshop time, consulting quietly with others, reading, and even drawing in order to get their words on the page? Do they think of writing time as only solitary and silent, or do they see choices appropriate to their own process?

- Have I planned opportunities for students to talk about their own writing processes? What might I do to help students feel comfortable enough with their own processes to discuss them with others? Have I scheduled enough time for talk during all parts of the writing process?

STANDARD 6: Students apply knowledge of language structure, language conventions, media techniques, figurative language, and genre to create, critique, and discuss print and nonprint texts.

GUIDING QUESTIONS

- Have I planned opportunities for students to practice conventions and craft in both short and long periods of time?
- Have I planned opportunities for students to choose genres appropriate to their purpose and audience?
- Have I planned opportunities for students to talk with others about their understanding of language structure, conventions, and figurative language? Can they serve as peer revision buddies when others in the class need support?

Summing Up

When we think of assessment only as something that happens at the end of instruction, we miss many opportunities to become more effective teachers. Here are some tips for effectively planning while considering assessment:

- Don't allow a prepackaged program to give you tunnel vision. If students are not improving as writers, look at the materials you are using and plan according to what students need, not what a program dictates.
- Search for the thinking required in your state standards or district benchmarks. Consider the process skills students will need to become successful writers. As you plan, do not just focus on the products students will have to create.
- When you plan, be flexible and intentional with how you use time, topic choice, and talk.

3

3

Feedback as Formative Assessment

few years ago while I was working with a group of eighth-grade students, I shared the rubric I was going to use to score their papers (see Figure 3.1). The rubric was meant to clarify my expectations, and I also wanted students to use the rubric as a self-assessment tool. After we scored a few sample papers I created so that I could determine how well my students understood the rubric, I asked them to score their own work for the next few weeks. Some students automatically gave themselves a 4 (advanced) without really examining their papers, while others spent more time determining their actual score. During the weeks I used the rubric I didn't really notice much improvement in some of the students' writing. Several students remained in the 2 range even though I was focusing my instruction on higher-level writing craft techniques. Students who consistently gave themselves 4's did not always meet my expectations; I tended to give many of these students lower scores, and the debating began.

Figure 3.1
Holistic Writing Rubric for the Short Constructed-Response Task, Grades 4–10

Score level	Content and Organization	Style and Fluency
4	• Supporting details are relevant and provide important information about the topic. • The writing has balance; the main idea stands out from the details. • The writer seems in control and develops the topic in a logical, organized way. • The writer connects ideas to the specified purpose.	• The writer selects words that are accurate, specific, and appropriate for the specified purpose. • The writer may experiment with and/or use figurative language and/or imagery. • The writer uses a variety of sentence structures. • The writing is readable, neat, and nearly error-free.
3	• The writer has defined but not thoroughly developed the topic, idea, or story line. • Some supporting details are relevant but limited or overly general or less important. • The writer makes general observations without using specific details or does not delineate the main idea from the details. • The writer attempts to develop the topic in an organized way but may falter in either logic or organization. • The writer connects ideas with the specified topic implicitly rather than explicitly.	• The writer mostly selects words that are accurate, specific, and appropriate for the purpose of the writing. • The writer uses age-appropriate words that are accurate but may lack precision. • The writer uses simple but accurate sentence structures. • Errors in language usage, spelling, and mechanics do not impede communication.
2	• The writer has defined but not thoroughly developed the topic, idea, or story line; response may be unclear or sketchy or may read like a collection of thoughts from which no central idea emerges. • Supporting details are minimal or irrelevant or no distinction is made between main ideas and details. • The writer does not develop the topic in an organized way; response may be a list rather than a developed paragraph. • Ideas are not connected to the specified purpose.	• The writer sometimes selects words that are not accurate, specific, or appropriate for the purpose of writing. • Writing may be choppy or repetitive. • Portions of the writing are unreadable or messy; errors may impede communication in some portions of the response.
1	• The writer has not defined the topic, idea, or story line. • Supporting details are absent. • Organization is not evident; may be a brief list. • Ideas are fragmented and unconnected with the specified purpose.	• Much of the writing is unreadable or messy. • Word choice is inaccurate or there are many repetitions. • Vocabulary is age-inappropriate. • The writer uses simple, repetitive sentence structures or many sentence fragments. • Errors severely impede communication.
0	• The response is off-topic or unreadable.	• The response is off-topic or unreadable.

Source: Colorado Department of Education (www.cde.state.co.us)

We all began to wonder if the rubric was working. It was supposed to make everything less subjective and more "fair" in their eyes, but the assessment piece was not working for many of us. My instructional decisions based on rubric scores did not seem to make a difference in many students' writing, and the final, summative scores caused too much debate. We were all spending too much time trying to make the rubric work rather than paying attention to our writing. We were lost.

I changed tactics one day to see what would happen: I decided to make a criteria list—a writing checklist—using student-friendly language based only on the descriptors for level 4 in the rubric (see Figure 3.2; also in appendix). In essence, I took away the possibility of students scoring any lower than a 4 by only showing the highest expectations. If they did not meet these expectations, then they had to leave the area next to the descriptor unchecked. Since I did not label the checklist with any numbers and just asked students to indicate if they met the criteria or not, I assumed students' self-assessments would align with my expectations.

When I handed out the checklist and began to explain how to use it, one of my students asked, "Where's the 2?"

I was confused at first. "What do you mean?"

He replied: "You know, the 2. It says I can write just a little bit, and it doesn't have to be very clear. I like the 2."

This student was teaching me something about rubrics: while they are meant to clarify expectations, they can be misused. This student seemed to be saying that as long as he didn't get a 1, he was fine with how his writing was progressing—or in my eyes, *not* progressing. Rubrics and checklists are *tools* for feedback, and when we are using them for summative or formative assessment purposes, we must be intentional or they may be as ineffective as a grade on top of a paper with no explanation.

Rubrics: Use and Misuse

I remember when I first heard about rubrics. I was in a staff development workshop in my district in the early 1990s, and we were learning about how to make assessment meaningful to students. Rubrics were touted as the answer. We were told to clearly define our expectations for students and to develop rubrics to describe various performance levels. Trainers provided sample rubrics, and we created some of our own based on work we had been doing with students at the time.

Figure 3.2

Writing Checklist

CONTENT AND ORGANIZATION

____ I included important details in my writing.

____ My writing has a clear main idea.

____ My writing is organized and logical: the ideas fit together.

____ My writing has a clear purpose.

STYLE AND FLUENCY

____ I used awesome words: specific nouns, descriptive adjectives, and strong verbs.

____ I used just the right amount of similes, metaphors, sensory details, or imagery to help make a picture in the reader's mind.

____ Some of my sentences are long, and some of them are short. Not all of my sentences begin with the same word.

____ I checked my writing for errors in spelling, capitalization, and punctuation.

My classroom suddenly exploded with rubrics. I had rubrics for everything from science labs to written explanations in math to research-based reports.

I tended to take rubrics very literally, so when I was given samples with a 4, 3, 2, 1 scale, I followed this model for everything I created. I even gave students a rubric for how their research-based projects looked on the page: a 4 had a pleasing font and eye-catching visuals, while a score of 3 might have a "somewhat pleasing font," and "interesting visuals."

The problems I had with rubrics were self-inflicted. I do not blame my training. Looking back, I see now that I was not creating rubrics on the most essential understandings in each subject area. I was creating rubrics for everything because my ultimate goal was to come up with a point-based grading system. In addition to creating too many rubrics, I found I became obsessed with finding the right adjectives to differentiate between a 1, 2, 3, and 4. I was spending more time developing "perfect" rubrics than I was planning for instruction. In the language of assessment, all of my thinking about rubrics was summative rather than formative, because my goal was to *grade*, not to *change my instruction* based on what students produced.

I still see rubrics that worry me because of the way they differentiate between a 1 and a 4, especially in regard to student writing. A student might receive a 4 if he or she uses three or more "exciting adjectives," while a 3 might mean the student uses "everyday" adjectives. Numbers often appear in such rubrics: a student who uses two similes and three sensory details receives a higher score than a student who includes only one simile and two sensory details. These rubrics imply that writing can be mathematically parsed for summative assessment purposes. We want to quantify because we feel less subjective if we assign everything a number. In the most extreme example of how rubrics can be misused, companies sell grading software that actually "scores" student writing by calculating sentence length and complexity. Surely Ernest Hemingway would receive low grades for writing if a computer software system did the scoring. He would undoubtedly receive a score of 1 on sentence variety and fluency. Where is the room for voice in such software? Where is the place for the unique, individual process each writer brings to the page when we so desperately want to make everything quantifiable?

The desire to make assessing student writing easier is what leads us to purchase software and use number-driven rubrics. I will be the first to admit that assessing writing is not easy—especially when working in middle or high school, where the paper load is daunting. How can we meaningfully support student achievement in writing when faced with more than 100 papers to read? And even in the primary grades, where teachers have fewer students, the process of looking for teaching points while examining each paper can be overwhelming. It is hard not to focus entirely on what students are *not* doing rather than on what they *are* doing well. One answer, I believe, is in using the tools we have in the writing workshop in formative, rather than just summative, ways.

The Danger of Focusing on a Single Score

While meeting with a group of teachers to establish common expectations for writing, it dawned on me that we might spend too much time focusing on a single score on a rubric rather than looking for instructional strategies to help move the student writing forward.

About thirty of us, grouped in clusters of three to five, looked at pieces created by seventh-grade students. The samples came from the Colorado Department of Education website (www.cde.state.co.us) and were released so that teachers could become more clear about expectations on our state test. The writing prompt follows:

> *Identify an animal that has gained a reputation—good or bad—based on popular beliefs. Then decide whether or not the reputation is deserved, and persuade the reader to agree with your reasoning.*

The samples we scored as a group follow. All student errors are kept intact:

Student Sample 1

There are many common animals that are supposed to bring good—or bad—luck to the owners. A back cat just crossed your path! Quick! Throw some salt over your shoulder! I really don't think it's worth the trouble, and

I'll tell you why . . . SILLY SUPERSTITIONS! Black cats have crossed my path numerous times. I have actually had great days!

One day my neighbor's coal-colored cat, Midnight, darted right in front of me as I walked to school. When I got to school, what did I find? Mayhem? Madness? No, I got 100% on a math test and no homework. If that's bad luck, I want some more! The only reason black cats are said to be bad luck is because back in the 17th century, it was noticed that an accused witch kept the company of a black cat. Soon these ebony creatures were associated with witches, and if it crossed your path you better watch out. So next time Blacky streaks by, smile and keep going.

Student Sample 2

A dog because it is mans best friend. More and more people are getting dogs for protection and comfort. The blind use dog for giudes. Cops use dogs for sniffing out drugs. Dogs are fun to play with. They only thing bad about owning a dog is the barking at night.

We spent about fifteen minutes debating whether each student scored a 4, 3, or 2 based on the rubric in Figure 3.1. While most teachers agreed that the first sample deserved a 4, some were concerned about the use of dashes, an ellipsis, and one-word sentences. The second paper caused more heated discussion. Many teachers scored the paper a 2, a few believed it was poor enough to deserve a 1, and one or two believed it should be scored a 3 because it did meet the bare requirements of the prompt. This means the student could either be marked proficient, partially proficient, or unsatisfactory. I worried about this discussion because if a student consistently scores below the proficient level in my district, then a learning plan must be developed, a parent conference is held, and interventions for the student are discussed. So what happened with the rubric? Rubrics are meant to clarify, not cause confusion. Did the problem come from the rubric itself, or from our use of the rubric?

We all decided both students had answered the prompt, and we agreed the second student needed to include more specific details. The advantage to the rubric was in how it focused our discussion on a common set of expectations for writing, but the disadvantages surfaced when teachers wanted to debate the actual score. The difficulty was compounded by the inevitable comparison to the first student's piece: even those who felt the first piece was proficient rather than advanced felt it was advanced *compared to the second sample.* So even when we use a rubric, it seems, there are "good" papers that receive a 4, and there are "great" papers that receive a 4. Many teachers decide to give the less-than-great papers a 3.5, and when that happens, we might as well just give these papers a B+ or an A- and forget the rubric altogether. In order to prevent some of this confusion, we need to think about how to most effectively use the rubrics as assessment tools.

Holistic rubrics designed to give only one score for writing are particularly difficult to use for informing instruction because the qualities of the writing are not separated out. When we use rubrics for the sole purpose of giving writing a single score, we are using these rubrics summatively. We aren't considering how the rubric might inform our instruction, which would be a formative use of this same scoring tool. I am proposing a more flexible use of rubrics as assessment tools.

In the case of the two earlier pieces, based on the rubric, we all agreed the second student stayed on the topic and provided some details to support the main idea. When we finally moved the conversation away from giving the piece one score, we engaged in a discussion about what the writer did well and how the writer could improve. We soon began discussing instructional strategies, and I think this is a crucial step in assessing student writing. I believe that even if a rubric is holistic, it is effective only if it leads to a discussion about teaching points. If we remain at the level of the score only, then we cannot move to where teachers do their work: in classrooms, making instructional choices about how to help students improve. Rubrics should be used flexibly as tools for instruction—not just as hammers for placing students in one permanent place.

The easiest way to remain flexible within the confines of a rubric is to highlight where the student is performing. On any given piece, three areas may be highlighted in the advanced descriptors, one or two in the proficient descriptors, and some may fall in the lower ranges on the rubric. But since my goal is to use the rubric *formatively* to guide my instruction rather than *summatively*, I have no problem with this: I can look at the highlighted areas to develop teaching points to increase student achievement.

If we use no rubrics at all, the danger of comparing can lead us astray. We may only think of how well our most advanced students are performing when we read student work, and in my experience, this is not only unfair but also damaging to learning. I call this student-to-student comparison "The Hannah Effect." Hannah is one of those students who comes along once or twice in a teacher's career. At age eleven, she truly was the most brilliant writer in the room the year she entered my fifth-grade class. Her writing made us laugh, cry, and learn, and we always wanted to hear more from her. When Hannah moved on to sixth grade, I missed her as the next year began. No one measured up to her, but I should not have compared my current students to her. Perhaps it is just human nature to compare in this manner, but even if it is, we need to be cautious, especially as teachers who care about the achievement of all of our students. No one was advanced *compared to Hannah,* but many of my students were advanced or proficient writers *compared to the standards* as outlined in the rubrics I used. It would be like putting me up against Tiger Woods during my first golf lesson; I should be compared against a standard, but not one that is solely based on the professional level. Students need to begin somewhere and improve from there—comparing them against only the best and not recognizing where they started makes assessment into a punishment, not a true measure of success.

What Do Students Think?

Rubrics have been around long enough for us to question their usefulness. Maja Wilson's fascinating book *Rethinking Rubrics in Writing Assessment* (2006) points to the many pitfalls of rubrics and how they can easily be misused. She effectively describes how we came to rely on them so heavily in the beginning of her book: "They promise to save time. They promise to boil a messy process down to four to six rows of nice, neat, organized little boxes. Who can resist their wiles? They seduce us with their appearance of simplicity" (2).

Vicki Spandel, who has advocated for the use of rubrics in a 6-Traits format for many years, has questioned the criticism of teachers and writers like Wilson: "When thoughtfully crafted and used with discretion and understanding, rubrics can be among the most useful instructional tools we have. They give us direction and a basis for conversation" (2006, 19). I think this is a very healthy debate. As I have stated, I am skeptical about rubrics, particularly those that encourage the counting of a certain number of specific types of figurative language or verbs. I think a balance is needed, and once again, I have found the best way to find out anything I want to know is to ask students themselves.

I cannot claim that my data is scientific, but the vast majority of students I have interviewed believe that rubrics help them to be better writers. In Pam Widmann's sixth- and seventh-grade classes at Liberty Middle School in Centennial, Colorado, students are encouraged to help her revise rubrics she has created based on her teaching objectives. I have often asked students to help me create rubrics in the past, but I found Pam's revision idea made the process not only much quicker, but much more meaningful.

I visited Pam's class when she was introducing the rubric for poems she asked students to write. She wanted students to focus on the sound devices commonly found in poetry—rhythm, rhyme, onomatopoeia, and alliteration. Students had read various examples of poems that used these devices, and they had written short drafts of poems to practice. She assigned them to write one poem about something that actually makes a sound. The second poem required students to describe something using sound devices. For example, Poem 1 might be about a tiger, and Poem 2 might be about happiness. Pam created the rubric in advance and brought it in for discussion (see Figure 3.3).

Figure 3.3
Poetry Rubric 1

VOICE	Above and Beyond		10
	Excellent	Precise, vivid vocabulary enhances meaning, paints strong images, and establishes mood	8.5 8
	Good	Communicates interest and passion for topics selected	7.5 7
	Average	Sounds like poetry (examples provided all week)	6.5 6
	Poor	Sounds like ordinary sentences	
FORMAT	Above & Beyond		10
	Excellent	Visuals add to impact of poem	8.5 8
	Good	Combined, the poem includes all poetic sound devices listed	7.5 7
	Average	• 6–15-line minimum each poem • Poem 1 topic is something that makes the sound described • Poem 2 topic is something that doesn't make a sound but is described with sound	6.5 6
	Poor	Missing poetic sound devices Cannot read	
MECHANICS/ CONVENTIONS Poetry allows author freedom with capitalization, punctuation, etc.	Above & Beyond		
	Excellent	No errors	5
	Good	1–2 errors	4.5
	Average	3–4 errors in spelling and mechanics that do not detract from meaning	4
	Poor	Too many errors in grammar and mechanics	3.5

One thing to keep in mind about this process of revising rubrics is that students may want to eliminate a section altogether. This happened immediately with Pam's students when they noticed the conventions section. "I don't want to be scored on conventions, because there are no conventions in poetry. We can break the rules," one student immediately piped up. When Pam and I explained that poetry actually does follow some conventions, the students understood and agreed. We compromised by eliminating the conventions category from the point total, but we kept it as a category for comments. This made sense for Pam's purpose: her goal was to make sure students could use the poetic devices, and since poetry is a genre which allows for different types of rules, we felt these conventions debates might actually get in the way as students wrote their poems.

We focused next on the format. Originally, Pam asked students to keep the poems between six and fifteen lines long. This caused many students discomfort: "What if I write a really long poem, but it is really good? Will I get a lower score just because it is long?"

Jenny even came to the defense of a boy who was known for his ability to write poems: "If Richard writes a great long poem, he shouldn't get a lower grade no matter what!"

The model poems we studied were short, and a majority of students agreed they would probably write very short poems, but they would not agree to limiting the number of lines in the rubric. So, Pam and I let it go. The new descriptor read: "Six-line minimum."

We all agreed the original requirement to use all the sound devices had to be changed, because a particular poem's purpose or subject might require the use of only some devices. If students were required to use all devices, the poems might be less authentic. The category about word choice was agreeable to students: they felt it was fine to score the writing on imagery and strong word choice, because this was the purpose of poetry. See Figure 3.4 for the final product students helped create.

Figure 3.4
Poetry Rubric 2

VOICE	Above and Beyond		5
	Excellent	Precise, vivid vocabulary enhances meaning, paints strong images, and establishes mood	4
	Good	Communicates passion for topics selected	3.5
	Average	Sounds unique (Doesn't sound like ordinary speech) (examples provided all week)	3
	Poor	Sounds like ordinary sentences	
FORMAT	Above & Beyond		5
	Excellent	The look of the poem on the page enhances the meaning of the poem	4
	Good	Sound devices used are appropriate to the purpose of poem	3.5
	Average	• 6-line minimum each poem • Poem 1 topic is something that makes the sound described • Poem 2 topic is something that doesn't make a sound but is described with sound	3
	Poor	Missing poetic sound devices Cannot read	
MECHANICS/ CONVENTIONS Poetry allows author freedom with capitalization, punctuation, etc.		TEACHER COMMENTS ONLY	

I am intentionally including a rubric discussion about poetry in this chapter because I believe it is the genre that is the most difficult to pigeonhole. If rubrics can lead to a reductive view of writing, is poetry not the most "dangerous" genre for rubric creation? And yet, the students had such rich comments about what they believed to be fair, and since Pam had exposed them to the types of poetry she wanted them to produce, the discussion was not about making poems easy to grade. Instead, we talked about how to make sure their best efforts were honored.

Pam always includes an "above and beyond" category in her rubrics because she wants students to know they can go outside the box. She does not ever want her students to think of writing as a formula to be followed, so her rubrics eliminate the impression that all writing follows some type of recipe. Sample poems from this assignment appear in Figures 3.5, 3.6, and 3.7.

I invite any criticism of the rubric we created collaboratively with the sixth graders. Debate is healthy, and we must remain slightly skeptical of our practices so we leave room to grow. But for those who would question ever using a rubric for poetry, I would also ask you to think about the discussion I just described. These students demonstrated knowledge not only of poetry but also of themselves as writers. Think about Jenny, who interrupted us to defend her classmate Richard because his poem should not be scored lower if it was long. If rubrics are meant to provide meaningful feedback, then who better to ask about the effectiveness of this feedback than the students in front of us?

These students demonstrated in-depth knowledge of the writing process and the genre of poetry. Are rubrics necessary to guide this type of thinking? No, certainly not. But the technique of bringing in a rubric for review certainly worked to bring the level of discussion to application and synthesis. Pam displayed the rubric, and the students immediately had something to say. And since rubrics categorize the language of writing into specific topics, we were all speaking the same language.

When used effectively, rubrics can help to provide a common language about writing. I do not believe it matters if this language is couched in the 6 Traits of writing or the qualities of writing found in other approaches to

Figure 3.5
Student poem from Pam's class

Books
by Daryn

Crisp pages break

Their way through

The vacant silence,

Like an awakening

Dawn, giving birth

To the first

Whir and

Hum of

Morning.

The book enters the

World at a slow pace,

To let the presence

Of each and every

Word be listened to,

Like a ray of golden

Sunlight piercing its

Way through a

Cloudy day.

Every Book Tries To Tell Us Something, We Just Have To Listen.

Figure 3.6
Student poem from Pam's class

Tumbling Thunder

by Renee

thunder can be strong
a warning
a sign
tumbling around all hope

inviting a great flash
of astounding light
it starts a melody of echo
all around

splitting trees
cry out in fear
of the fury that
will soon strike

when the entire world is calm
and all lamenting stops
you will know
that thunder has shuffled on

the thunder's ramble will
always cease
but the trance
will carry on

Figures 3.7
Student poem from Pam's class

Wind

by Megan

Singing sweet ballads the

Drizzling wind

Recognizes

The feeble, tired trees:

Pending the shadows of a frigid,

Abandoned, dreary night.

writing instruction. But I do believe it is helpful to have discussions in which a common vocabulary is used. When I think back to my continuous problem with passive voice in my own writing, it all came down to language. I wasn't sure what my high school teachers meant when they told me about my tendency to use passive voice. In Pam's class, and in dozens of classes like hers at all grade levels, I am struck by how clearly students begin to understand how to make their writing better because they speak the same language. One way to get there is to have frequent discussions, and for many teachers, well-constructed rubrics can help students to become even more clear about how to make their writing stronger.

The bottom line? As with so many issues in education, the tool is not the problem or the solution. Great tools can be misused, and marginal tools can elevate thinking in a well-run classroom. Teachers like Pam expect their students to think critically, and I know Pam can make even a marginal rubric sing when she asks for student input.

Conferences: An Assessment Lens

Classroom discussions like the one described in the last section can provide a general feel for how the class is coming along with a particular concept or idea. When I ask a class to notice things about one another's writing or about professional writing, I can listen to develop teaching points. Another place to do this kind of listening is during a conference.

The best ideas I have read about conferring with students are in Carl Anderson's book *How's It Going?* (2000). He recommends that we listen to students read their work and then take a research stance—we should think of something we can teach the student about his or her piece of writing that can be used later in other writing. I completely agree with Carl. As teachers of writing, we are primarily researchers, trying to figure out exactly what we need to teach our students as they share their work with us. I want to add that I think we can also learn a lot about what students need from an assessment standpoint if we listen to what they say about their own writing processes during these conferences.

In preparation for conferring with Sharon Miller's second-grade class, I read student work in advance. I wanted to get a picture of the types of writers I was going to be working with, and the easiest way for me to do this was to read their writing. I only had to read a few pieces to get a clear picture of what Sharon had been teaching in her writing workshop. I read pieces that demonstrated a clear sense of storytelling, and strong verbs and descriptive adjectives punctuated many of the students' pieces. When I read student work, I notice something to praise, I look for something to wonder about, and then I look for teaching points. I think preparing for conferences with students and actually listening to them while the conference is occurring provide some of the most authentic opportunities to assess student writing.

When I talked with Kay, for example, I had no doubts she knew what tools were available to her as a writer. Her piece about an accident at school began with a strong lead: an image of a straight, quiet line of students heading to PE, unaware of the upcoming "disaster." She was setting the reader up to wonder what was going to happen, and later on she described how she fell and skinned her knee on the way to PE and how a friend helped her to the nurse's office. Kay's skinned knee constituted a "disaster" in her mind because she missed her favorite class due to an unexpected injury.

When I read this piece prior to the conference, I knew I would comment on the lead, but I also had a question. "I wonder how you thought to start your piece this way, Kay. I have this image of a straight, quiet line, and you make me want to read on because of this great word 'disaster.' How did you think of this?"

"Because of my writing buddy," she responded.

"Tell me about that."

"My writing buddy is Hogan. When he read my story, he said I should add more details. He asked me questions about the line—'Was it a straight line? Was it noisy?'—and that helped me to start my story."

In these few comments, I learned so much: Kay knew how to make her writing better, and she made the decision to change her piece so that the lead would draw the reader in. She got the suggestion from someone else, but she decided to take up the suggestion and she used the idea effectively.

I also learned something about Hogan. He was able to give advice to his buddy. Hogan's own writing was trickier than Kay's to understand—he developed a snowboard-hovercraft product idea he wanted to send to Sony. His writing was a mix of a persuasive letter, a how-to manual, and a description of how fun it would be to ride on his invention.

But I knew something about Hogan I didn't know from just reading his piece: he knew strong, descriptive leads can enhance writing, and he knew how the right lead can make the reader anticipate what is to come. I praised Hogan for helping his buddy Kay with her lead before I talked about his piece, which I think established a positive tone for me to begin our conference.

When we turned to his piece, I began with a question. "Tell me about this piece. Your new invention is so interesting. Can you tell me more about it?"

Hogan pointed to his pictures and diagrams, and what he said made perfect sense. He had a clear picture in his mind and in diagrams about the product he wanted to invent. My teaching points for him were about organization. I suggested he number all his pictures and then number the writing he had already done, matching the text to the pictures. Once he began this process, he had a stronger sense of where to go.

So, from listening to his writing buddy, I knew Hogan had a strong sense of how to begin stories, and from working with him, I learned he organized his writing through ideas and diagrams. He was working in a complex structure, so if I were to assess him, I would not say that he was unable to organize his thinking—comments from his writing buddy, and even from his own work, proved otherwise—but that he might need support for creating a clear vision of what he might want to do with his piece. Once that was clear, the writing became easier. While my teaching points for Kay might come after she begins her piece, my teaching points for Hogan might need to come earlier, because he struggled with organization as soon as he began his draft. When he spoke to me about his drawing, he had great ideas, but once the words began to flow, it was difficult to follow his line of thinking. Hogan might be a student I would always talk to prior to when he began his writing, because once we talked, I was convinced he was more clear about how he might approach his piece. From just these two short conversations, I had begun to develop a sense of what I might need to do instructionally to meet students' needs.

Linking Conferences and Assessment

So, if you were conferring with me right now, would you ask: "What are these ideas doing in a book on assessment of writing? What about grades and standards and proficiency ratings? Is Hogan below proficiency level because he was unable to organize his own piece independently?"

All of these questions are valid.

We live in a public education system that is hungry to post scores. So how do we align the push for scoring writing with the idea of conferences like the ones I just described?

I believe we must base our decisions about proficiency levels on data. But I think this data can come from multiple sources. Perhaps because of state testing mandates, many teachers I work with base student performance ratings on writing that is completed independently, often from common, schoolwide prompts. This is especially true in upper elementary and middle school classrooms I work in. The danger in gathering data so divorced from instruction is that it can lead to ineffective, disconnected teaching, as pointed out in the *Educational Leadership* article "Classroom Assessment: Minute by Minute, Day by Day":

> *In a classroom that uses assessment to support learning, the divide between instruction and assessment blurs. Everything students do—such as conversing in groups, completing seatwork, answering and asking questions, working on projects, handing in homework assignments, even sitting silently and looking confused—is a potential source of information about how much they understand. The teacher who consciously uses assessment to support learning takes in this information, analyzes it, and makes instructional decisions that address the understandings and misunderstandings that these assessments reveal. (Leahy, Lyon, Thompson, and Wiliam 2005, 19)*

The description of formative assessment in this article shows how a teacher who is considering all data points—all information—to support learning can more effectively manage instruction. One of the key recommendations in the article is that students be instructional resources for one another, just like Hogan was a resource for Kay in Sharon Miller's classroom, described in the last section.

When Kay sought support from her writing buddy, she was demonstrating her knowledge about how to effectively access support as a writer. When Hogan gave his writing buddy Kay meaningful advice about her lead, he was demonstrating his knowledge about writing craft techniques. Kay's seeking support and Hogan's advice can be used as data to determine how these second graders are growing as writers.

Keeping Track of Data

If one of the goals of this book is to provide alternatives to grading and to think of other ways to monitor student progress, how can we keep track? If I am going to use data gathered from my conversations with students to prove where they are as writers, how am I going to record and save this data?

One way is through anecdotal notes. Prior to conferring with students, I make sure that I have all students' names written down so that I can easily record my thinking next to their names. Remember what I learned about Hogan when I talked with Kay, since he was her writing buddy? I recorded my quick thinking next to Hogan's name: I wrote *lead*, for example, as an indication that he had a sense of a strong lead. When I actually met with Hogan, I added my teaching points or concerns to these shorthand notes.

I recommend carrying a chart with students' names as you walk around the room checking on how students are doing. Not all conferences need to be in a separate space from the rest of the group. I can learn from all my conversations with writers, and if I keep a list of names with me, I can quickly record what I notice.

This type of assessment chart can also be used for note taking while students share. After a student shares his or her piece, I can listen carefully to other students' comments to assess how well they have internalized the qualities of good writing. If they are able to praise their classmates' writing for strong leads, active verbs, and imagery, for example, then I know that they are more likely to produce this type of writing on their own. I can also call on specific students during the debriefing times to see if they have begun to show an understanding of how to comment on one another's work.

Charting comments and notes on how students are progressing can be a valuable tool for assessment purposes. I will discuss grades later, but creating data is something I believe we must move to if we want to become more effective teachers. One paper a week from students will not provide the same rich data that notes from conversations will. More tools for keeping track of student conferences will be shared in Chapter 6.

Summing Up

Though rubrics can be useful tools for examining student work, there are some ways to misuse use them that may prevent us from helping students to become better writers. Here are some tips to prevent the misuse of rubrics:

- If you cannot decide what to score a student within a few minutes of using a rubric, then either look for logical teaching points within the rubric, or read the piece with no rubric and see what stands out.

- Abandon the search for the perfect rubric. If a rubric can help to guide you as you monitor student progress, it is good enough. No rubric can answer all student needs.

- Don't overdo it with rubrics. If you create a rubric, include only the most essential elements in the content, and allow room for surprise.

- Ask students to help you in creating rubrics or in revising existing rubrics to make them more student friendly. If a rubric cannot be used to clarify expectations, then it is not as useful as it could be.

- Ask students for consistent, honest feedback about how rubrics are helping them as writers and as readers of peer work. If you sense that the rubric is limiting discussions in your classroom about good writing, then talk to students about how important it is to react to a piece honestly.

- Challenge students to find examples of strong writing in their own work and in professional work that may not fit perfectly into a rubric. This will help all of you work together to either alter the rubric or understand that sometimes, writing just "works," rubrics or not. We have countless examples of masterful writing that exist outside the realm of rubrics.

- Use data from conferences and discussions to create a broader picture of how students are performing as writers.

4

4

Self-Assessment

Within a few minutes of visiting with Brad Ayres and Cindy Meyers's kindergarten students at Polton Elementary in Aurora, Colorado, it dawned on me that five- and six-year-olds seem to be more self-aware about their writing than many older students. While it is true that primary students often ask for help with spelling and mechanics, they also display a certain joy in sharing what they know about everything: from dinosaurs to pet dogs to taking care of a newborn baby sister, they long to tell adults what they know.

And these kindergarten students knew a lot about writing. They told me writers must first think to come up with an idea, and that they often draw before they write, but only if they want to. "I draw *after* I write," one girl proudly noted.

They told me writers need to remember the rules about capitals, periods, and spaces between words. When I asked what writers should do if they weren't sure how to spell a word, they confidently stated: "You stretch it out and do the best you can."

As I watched these students write, I was impressed by their independence. Some were walking up to the word wall for spelling support. Others were stretching out words, sounding out each phoneme, and checking the alphabet charts taped to their desks. Some used fingers to place spaces between words, others used popsicle sticks, and one student called me over so I could watch how she did not use any tools for spacing because she *just remembered*.

I have been in other primary classrooms and witnessed students confidently searching their own personal dictionaries for just the right word or asking for help spelling a word not because they would otherwise have avoided the word, but because they wanted to put it in their personal dictionary spelled correctly. These same students might try another word they do not know how to spell in their writing and not ask for it to be placed in their dictionary, because they have the sense that they may not need this word very often. The personal dictionary is a place for words that might be used again—for words that are special and worth repeating. All of this self-knowledge lives in the minds of five- and six-year-olds.

What Happens After the Primary Grades?

When I reflect on my years teaching upper elementary and middle school, and when I visit classrooms now, I am struck by the difference in the ability of students to self-assess and use writing tools independently. A typical question from a first grader is, "Can I read you my story?" while a middle school student is more likely to ask, "Is this what you mean?" or "Is this good?" And, too often, they might ask: "Do we *have* to write?"

While it easily could be argued that primary students are writing less complex texts, I also believe that our youngest students have a lot more to think about while they write than students in the upper grades. Primary students are still actively thinking about the physical mechanics of writing while they are forming ideas. Regardless of the reason or the age, *students* are an integral part of the assessment process. My ultimate goal as a teacher is, in one sense, to work myself out of the job of being the sole "owner" of all knowledge. We should engender as much independence as we can. When I use the terms *independence* and *self-assessment*, I am not trying to conjure up images of students working in quiet rows, dutifully and silently drafting, revising, and editing. Instead, I envision classrooms where students know, select, and use the resources they need to improve as writers. Sometimes, the students will need the teacher to read over a piece. At other times, a student may need to run an idea by a peer or read a well-written book to gain insights into a professional writer's craft. A classroom setting where self-assessment happens is truly a workshop, and it will be full of activity.

Setting Product Goals for Writing

In the writing classroom, a logical place to begin when we want our students to become more independent is to ask them to set goals for their writing. Goal setting allows students to demonstrate what they know about themselves as writers, and goals aligned with this knowledge can provide opportunities for growth.

I visited Jan DiSanti's and James Shipp's fourth-grade classrooms at Eastridge Elementary in Aurora, Colorado, to talk about goal setting. We began by asking someone to share her writing so we could model what we meant when we asked them to set goals.

Franny volunteered to share a notebook entry about working as a tutor for a struggling second grader. When I asked her what she was proud of, Franny replied, "I am proud of helping a second grader learn how to read." Franny focused first on the subject matter of the piece, and we decided writers should choose topics meaningful to them. When I asked her to share what she was proud of in her writing, Franny showed the class her entry so they could see the genre: she had written a graphic novel, or comic strip, to depict her tutoring sessions. She said she was proud of herself for trying something different, and she mentioned how a boy in her class had been working on entries like these and he had inspired her to try. We moved to goals next. "What goals do you have for your writing?" I asked. Franny looked at her piece again and noticed the story she told out loud about tutoring was much richer than what she had written and drawn. She said, "My goal is to add more details."

Franny was able to create a goal for herself based on what real writers are concerned with: they do think of details while they write and often revise by adding more details or deleting unnecessary ones. In classrooms full of product-oriented talk, my experience has been that students can set meaningful goals for themselves. They may consider how effectively they use leads, word choice, organization, or specific details. The types of goals students identify will be based on the ongoing talk in the writing classroom.

Goals in Action

Once goals are set, then what? I worked for many years in a middle school where all conferences were based on student goals. I support empowering students during conferences to discuss their own learning, but sometimes the goal-setting process is tricky. One of the difficulties comes from how we talk with students about goals. Goal setting often breaks down when we confuse the goal with actions for reaching the goal. If I make a goal to eat healthier food, my plan for this is often just a restatement of the goal: I will eat more healthy food. My plan for getting more exercise is to—surprise, surprise—get more exercise. Students often mimic what they hear adults in their lives doing when they are asked how they might achieve their goals.

Franny, the fourth-grade student who decided she wanted to improve her writing products by adding details, said she would accomplish this by adding details. I wanted to make sure to clearly separate the difference between a goal and a plan of action, so when Franny said she would add more details, I opened up the discussion to the whole class. I asked them to think about a goal they had set for themselves and reached. Some students thought of sports they had improved in, and others thought about musical instruments they had learned how to play. It wasn't until I asked them who played video games that I engaged all students in this discussion of setting goals. "Who plays video games?" I asked. Nearly every hand in the room shot up. "And how many of you have improved in your ability to play these games?" Every hand stayed up. "*How* did you do it?" Finally, ideas poured in:

- Practice/rehearse
- Ask a friend for help

- Read about it
- Know the rules and tricks
- Try again
- Try to be faster

As the list became longer, the ideas for how to reach goals became more apparent to students. They each chose an area for improvement in their writing, and then they picked a method for reaching their goals. Franny, along with many other students, decided to ask friends for help because they already had writing partners in their classrooms.

If we want students to set meaningful goals and to practice meaningfully to meet these goals, then we must gather information about their processes as well as their products. Processes help us meet goals because they require *action*. The key to helping students improve as writers may have less to do with their writing products and more to do with how efficiently and effectively they create these products. Recall the observation in the beginning of this chapter that some primary students seem so much more independent than older students. I believe that the reason for this may have to do with how aware we are of young students' processes. When I taught intermediate students, I did not think much about students' processes during writing time, because even though we wrote a lot, I was paying more attention to the product. My conferences with students were based on content as it appeared on the page, or content as described by students.

It only takes a few minutes in a primary classroom to learn a lot about students' writing processes, because it is happening right in front of you and it is so physical—students are accessing word walls, choosing the right pencil, picking up their writer's folders or notebooks, talking quietly with friends, and sounding out words. In my own intermediate and middle school classrooms, because writing was less physical, I did not know as much about my writers.

Two student pieces of writing of equal quality sitting side by side on my desk at the end of the day only tell part of the story. How long did it take each student to write each piece? Did each of the students plan prior to writing, or did they just begin writing? Did they think for a long time prior to beginning, or did they dive right in and complete the piece in a short time period? One way to find out about processes is to watch students while they write, and the other is to ask them.

In Pam Widmann's sixth-grade class, we asked students to list these parts of the writing process:

- Getting ready to write/Idea making
- Writing/Drafting
- Revising/Editing

Then we asked students to think about themselves in each context. Because we knew this would be easier if they also thought about what didn't work, we asked them to create a two-column chart to record their thoughts (see Figure 4.1; also in appendix). After they had time to record their thoughts in each section, we asked them to set goals for their writing.

Mick knows his process inside out: he makes a web prior to writing a story and then imagines "how the story will come out according to my style of writing," yet he admits that, once the plan is done, he does not refer back to it while he writes. In the revising section he notes "[I] don't like being rushed," and he indicates he does not rely on friends to help him revise. His goals connect directly to his reflections, and he plans to "spend more time" in order to improve. (Mick chose not to use the two-column format and instead organized his thoughts under one column labeled "Details"; see Figure 4.2.)

Ana likes to talk to a friend while planning and getting ready to write. She does not use a written plan at all to get ready—her needs are met by talking with others in all stages of the process. Though she notes that "talking to no one" does not work for her as she writes, it is interesting that Ana creates a goal to be more independent: "My goals are to memorize my revision checklist so that I will become better with just tiny things that really effect my grades" (see Figure 4.3).

Figure 4.1
My Writing Process form

MY WRITING PROCESS		
	What works for me	What doesn't work
Getting ready to write/Idea making		
Writing/Drafting		
Revising/Editing		
Goals		

Figure 4.2
Mick's reflections on writing process

Main Ideas	Details
1) idea making getting ready to write	I always make a web' and then imagine how the story will come out according to my style of writing and edit the plot to make it an exciting story
2) writing	extend from plan to make the idea of the story better noise helps not to close to somebody quickwrite don't refer to plan
3)	revise on my own friends don't always help revise in red add better descriptors don't like being rushed like more time to revise the draft read backwards
4) Goal setting	this year in writing I'm proud of my narrative but I'm not very good at mechanics and saying what I mean right. I'm an average writer my goal this year is to spend more time on my writing

Figure 4.3
Ana's reflections on writing process

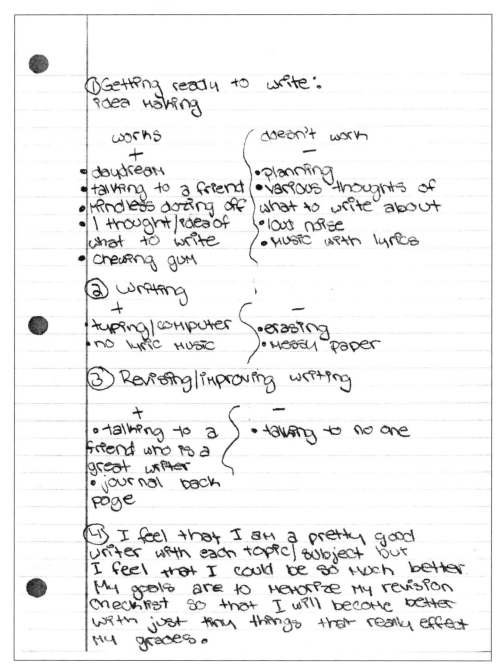

This opportunity to reflect helped all of Pam's students to identify their own processes, and it also gave Pam and me many windows of opportunity for teaching. It allowed us all to speak the same language, not only about writing products but also about how these products come to be.

Practice Day

Once students have set goals and have made plans for how to reach these goals, how can we organize our classrooms to help students assess their progress? One way is to set aside time to allow students individually to work on their goals as they write each day, perhaps by starting with a quick conference with the teacher or a peer to discuss what could be accomplished in a class period or a week. Another way to structure the workshop is to actually provide specific time, space, and materials for students to focus on practice.

Pam Widmann's sixth graders helped to design a day of practice after they developed their methods for reaching their goals. We asked them to think of ways they could practice in class, and told them that we would provide them the opportunity to meet their goals.

Each student filled out a "What and How" sheet, which listed what they planned to practice followed by a specific how. They were asked to give us a list of specific needs in order to implement their plans so that we could adequately prepare for this opportunity to practice.

Many of the students who wanted to practice writing craft techniques asked for various types of models, so Pam and I collected newspaper articles, magazines, and novels for students to read during practice time. Several other students asked for "boring" writing samples that they could revise. We decided these students could create their own dull models and then revise them to make them more interesting. Some students asked for more time to "daydream" or think prior to writing, and others asked for a limited time to write because their goals involved creating stronger writing in a short period of time. Finally, many students asked for time to work with their peers on writing—they wanted time to read and discuss each other's work.

Pam and I examined student requests in advance, gathered materials, and created spaces in the library for each type of practice. As students filed in on Practice Day, we briefly explained the available options. Though they had signed up for a specific type of practice, we allowed students to self-select the kind of work they would do during the practice period. If students determined that a different type of practice would support their goals, they were free to move to a different practice station.

One group worked on leads, another on conclusions, and some worked together to peer edit and revise. Several students chose to work on grammar skills on the computer, while others worked on descriptive writing using picture cues. Some students used picture books to develop their writing craft.

Students could move from one station to another as they needed. The goal was to help students improve their own writing—to self-assess—so if one station would be more helpful, we encouraged them to move.

Some students benefited immediately. After looking at several *National Geographic Kids* magazines, one student found four different ways to end her piece. Another student found equal success by looking at only one page of Cynthia Rylant's beautiful homage to fall, *In November* (2000).

Some students struggled a bit to find their place—one student was stuck for quite a while at the lead table. When I asked her what she was working on, she said, "I don't want to change the lead of this piece," and after I read what she had written, I could see why. She began a piece about who she might choose to travel to another planet with using this lead: "Houston. We have a problem. I am traveling to Saturn and I can take only one friend."

I told her she did not need to change the lead—that it was her choice to work on whatever it was that might help her writing.

The table of timed writers was perhaps the most interesting. Though I am not an advocate of timed writing, it was fascinating to watch how many students chose to challenge themselves to get words on the page in the shortest amount of time possible. Pam had provided a series of prompts to respond to, and some students chose to use a picture to describe.

All the students who timed themselves left being very proud of how much they had written, and they were also impressed by the quality of their writing. Of all the practice stations, this one reminded me the most of the joy I see in primary classrooms: the students from this group could not wait to share their successes.

I am not suggesting all students can benefit from timed writing. But as a confidence builder, when offered as a choice, it was completely successful for several of these sixth graders.

I am also not suggesting that this separate practice period is the only structure that will work in a well-functioning writing workshop. In fact, I think a good workshop is full of this kind of meaningful practice on a daily basis. This idea just grew from our discussions with students, and there were some benefits to making the idea of practice as distinct, in both time and space, as we could. It provided students a real opportunity to reflect on themselves as writers.

Students Reflect on Their Practice

Pam and I asked students to write reflections about their work on Practice Day as a form of self-evaluation. Some students clearly benefited from the practice sessions. While some chose to use the time to revise an existing piece, others saw the practice as an opportunity to strengthen their skills in new writing.

Alani saw the practice as an opportunity to impact her future writing, but what she ended up practicing changed after she started her work. "At first I wanted to work on verbs and mechanics," she said, "but I realized I needed to work on conclusions and figurative language." Alani joined a table of students who had *Sports Illustrated for Kids* magazines and various picture books that featured figurative language. Though these sources also had strong verbs, the strong conclusions in the magazine articles and the use of figurative language in the books made her rethink her original strategy.

This is a good example of how models might be used differently, depending on the purpose. Alani was very clear that she wanted to use these books for a specific purpose: "[I practiced] by reading books and mirroring what they did but *not copying*" (emphasis mine). So often I read to students models of good writing by both professional authors and other students, but I don't always make it clear *how* these models might be used. Alani knows one way: by mirroring a style, but not copying it.

Based on her new ideas from the practice, Alani added this conclusion to an existing piece about a place she loved: "In this place, at the sun's mercy, the sand is steaming. The palm trees are friends to my fair skin. And the waves reach for the shore, with all their might, til finally they give in."

While some students stayed focused on one station, others wandered to many stations. These students effectively self-assessed—they knew if something was working or not, and they decided to move if the original task did not meet their needs. Zoe was one such student. She was most impressed with her progress after she visited the figurative language station and then challenged herself at the timed writing station. She wrote in her reflection about how impressed she was with the writing she produced in only six minutes. Zoe was not the only student who was surprised by the products created in her practice writing time. Megan sat at a "zoom" table, where dozens of pictures were provided, along with paper, for zooming in on specific details in writing. Each time a student rewrites about a picture at this station, he or she is encouraged to keep zooming in on smaller and smaller details. After her work, Megan wrote: "I am able to focus on things I would never have imagined," showing that she began to use this self-assessment and practice time to prove to herself that she could get better at writing. She may have found a tool she did not know she had at her disposal: the ability to zoom in closely. Here is a sample of her writing developed from a picture of fireworks over a lake:

First image:
The fireworks explode over the lake.

Second image:
The colorful fireworks glisten over the dazzling lake and quiet town.

Final image:
Multicolor explosions propel into the twilight, putting the only sound deep inside the hushed town.

While one could argue that Megan might be overusing descriptive language, I think it is important to keep in mind that these students were engaged in *practice*. Megan is trying new craft techniques, which is the purpose of the exercise.

Jen connected her practice to her goals in this way: "In the timed writings, I am not going to stop and wait until I think of a good idea, but I am just going to go for zooms. I am going to get as detailed as possible to get a vivid image."

Not all students felt they benefited from this practice time. Isaiah wrote, "I set goals on mechanics, figurative language, and timed writing during my practice time. I didn't learn much of anything. However, I did learn that I was already good enough at timed writing."

This is an interesting comment, because while Isaiah did not seem to benefit from looking at the same books for figurative language ideas that many students benefited from, he did notice that he was better at something than he originally thought—timed writing.

Mick mentioned that the practice helped him to get "unstuck." He already knew a lot about strong writing on the basis of his samples, but he improved them even more after working on leads and stronger verbs. In a piece about his favorite place, he effectively changed his lead:

Mick's Original Lead

My favorite place that has so many weird and absolutely unimaginable things happening in every single day is Hogwarts School of Wizardry

Mick's Revised Lead

Mysteriously shaded from us, Hogwarts School of Wizardry and witch craft is the place to be.

Again, what is interesting here is Mick's sense that he could make something he had written even better. He had written a clear lead, but after reading professional samples, he chose a more complex sentence structure to begin his piece.

Students Reflect on Their Achievement

Once students have set goals, had opportunities to practice, and written and revised a number of pieces, it is important to ask them to reflect on their achievement. Though writing is a process above all else, because students are in school, they are often subject to frequent progress reports. A more thorough discussion of grades follows in Chapter 5, but here, I want to discuss some possibilities for using self-assessment when asking students to reflect on their achievement.

At the end of a reporting period at Eastridge Elementary, James Shipp, Jan DiSanti, and I asked fifth-grade students to look through their writing folders and notebooks for evidence of their progress in writing. We provided them with an organizing framework (see Figure 4.4; also in appendix) and explained that they should name pieces they had created that represented their best efforts so far in each listed area. We based this framework on the language arts standards for Colorado and on the rubric used to score student writing on the state test. Students were welcome to use one piece of writing as a multiple indicator of success. For example, a student could use one story as evidence of a clear main idea, supporting details, and word choice.

While many students used their best pieces to prove their proficiency at many levels, I was struck in my conversations with students about how self-aware they were regarding their writing. Tristin was one such student. To demonstrate his ability to write with a clear main idea and supporting details, he chose a quick write about wanting to be a tiger (see Figures 4.5 and 4.6). When I asked Tristin about the strengths of this piece, he focused on the details: he had included much specific information about the tiger, and he also provided the reader with reasons for why he would choose to be a tiger. When I asked him why he did not use this piece as an example for meeting the

Figure 4.4
My Writing Progress form

MY WRITING PROGRESS

Name _____

CONTENT AND ORGANIZATION

My writing has a clear main idea.

1. _____   2. _____   3. _____

I included important details in my writing.

1. _____   2. _____   3. _____

My writing is organized and logical: the ideas fit together.

1. _____   2. _____   3. _____

Figure 4.4 (continued)

STYLE AND FLUENCY

I used awesome words:
- specific nouns
- descriptive adjectives
- and strong verbs

1. _____   2. _____   3. _____

I used just the right amount of
- similes,
- sensory details,
- or imagery to help make a picture in the reader's mind

1. _____   2. _____   3. _____

I wrote some long sentences, and some short sentences. Not all of my sentences begin with the same word.

1. _____   2. _____   3. _____

I have almost no errors in
- capitalization
- punctuation
- spelling

1. _____   2. _____   3. _____

organization standard, Tristin said, "It could be more organized. The details aren't really in order." After this brief discussion, Tristin went back to his notebook and folder to choose pieces that would demonstrate his proficiency in other areas.

Angelica demonstrated this same awareness in her comic piece "Booger" about her pet dog (see Figures 4.7 and 4.8). She chose this piece as proof that she can use descriptive words and varied sentence lengths while she writes. Angelica did not choose this piece to demonstrate a clear main idea because she felt she focused more on word choice while writing about her pet.

Asking students to assess their own progress helps the teacher determine what students have internalized. Students must clarify what they know about the quality of writing products in order to choose pieces that demonstrate how effectively they meet the standards. In very short conversations with students about their pieces, the teacher can get a clear picture of who has reached an independent level in the area of identifying strong writing products.

Summing Up

When students effectively self-assess, we all benefit. Students who know where they are and what they need in order to improve can help create a classroom environment where everyone is able to ask for the type of support he or she needs.

Some ideas to support this kind of environment include:

- Ask your students to self-assess their writing processes and products on a regular basis. When they focus on specific areas for improvement, we can more easily monitor their progress.
- Ask students for ideas about how they might practice in order to improve. This will lead to more meaningful practice that will support achievement.
- Provide specific practice times in class that support student-identified needs.
- Ask students to reflect on their progress often so that they can keep track of how they are doing.

Figure 4.5
Tristin's Writing Progress form

My Writing Progress

Name **Tristin**

CONTENT AND ORGANIZATION

My writing has a clear **main idea**.

1. The whisper   2. ultimate allience   3. _____

I included **important details** in my writing.

1. tiger   2. The whisper   3. _____

My writing is **organized and logical**: the ideas fit together.

1. _____   2. _____   3. _____

Figure 4.6
Tristin's writing sample

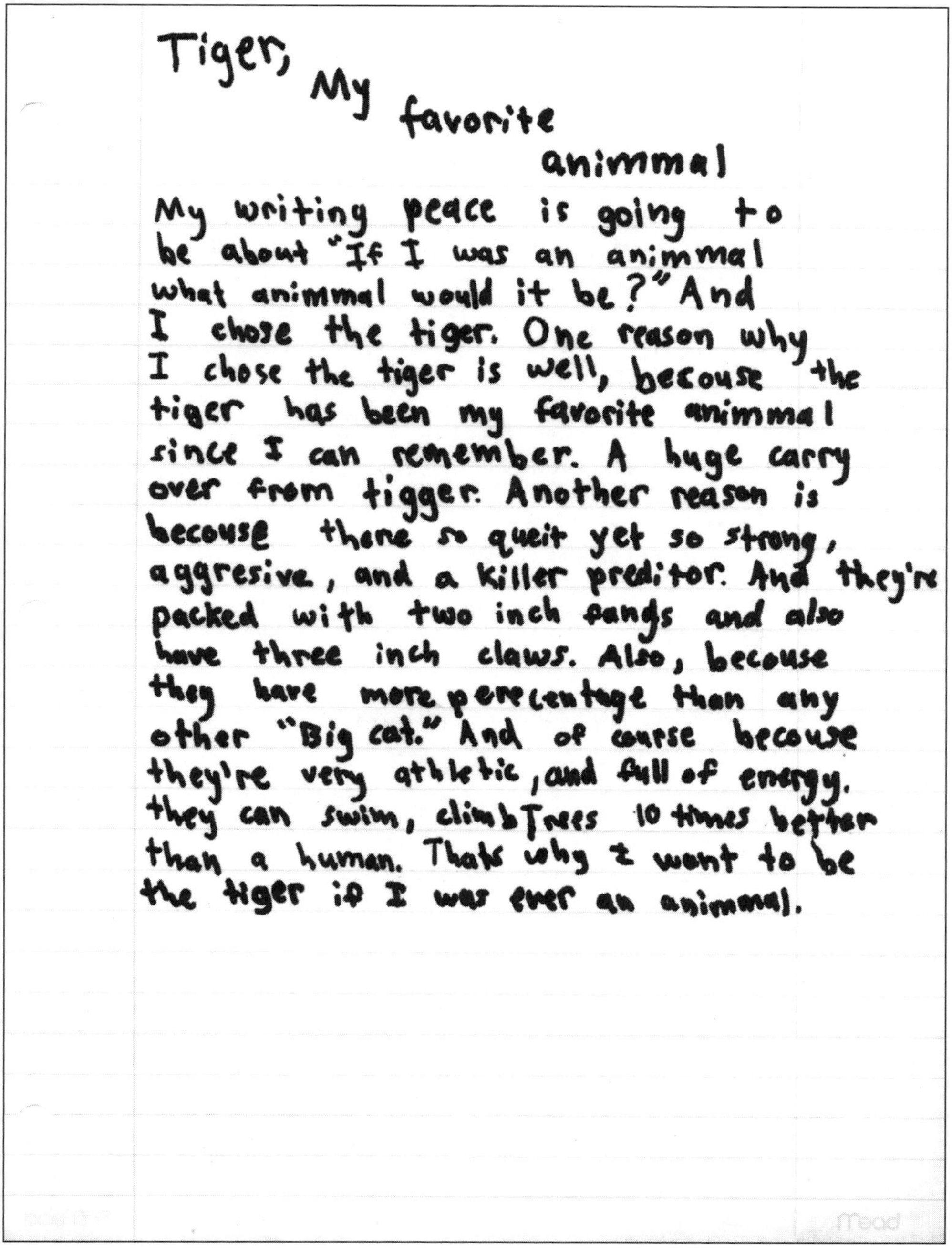

Tiger, My favorite animmal

My writing peace is going to be about "If I was an animmal what animmal would it be?" And I chose the tiger. One reason why I chose the tiger is well, becouse the tiger has been my favorite animmal since I can remember. A huge carry over from tigger. Another reason is becouse there so queit yet so strong, aggresive, and a killer preditor. And they're packed with two inch fangs and also have three inch claws. Also, becouse they have more percentage than any other "Big cat." And of course becouse they're very athletic, and full of energy. they can swim, climb Trees 10 times better than a human. Thats why I wont to be the tiger if I was ever an animmal.

Figure 4.7
Angelica's Writing Progress form

STYLE AND FLUENCY

I used awesome words:
- **specific nouns**
- **descriptive adjectives**
- and **strong verbs**

1. Booger   2. Dragonflies   3. Bumblebees

I used **just the right amount** of
- **similes,**
- **sensory** details,
- or **imagery** to help make a picture in the reader's mind

1. Comic Doodles   2. Model Material   3. September

I wrote **some long sentences,** and **some short sentences.** Not all of my sentences begin with the same word.

1. Model Material   2. Pinky   3. Booger

CONVENTIONS

I have **almost no errors** in
- capitalization
- punctuation
- spelling

1. Dragonflies   2. Booger   3. Pinky

Figure 4.8
Angelica's writing sample

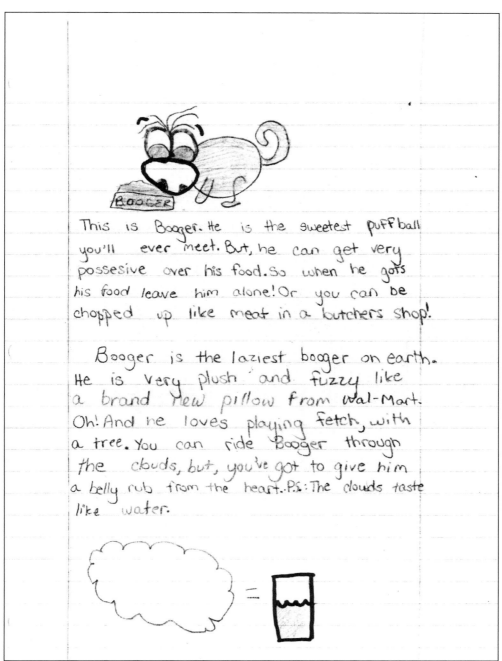

5

5

Grades

I took a visual arts course when I was an undergraduate. Just as I had virtually no experience with dance prior to going to the Martha Graham School in New York City when I first started teaching, I had not spent much time thinking about visual arts until I took this course that happened to fit into my schedule. I was interested in art but had never actually created any.

For the first assignment, we were asked to produce a small painting. I spent about ten hours over the weekend painting something that I cannot specifically recall—the only thing I remember about it is the professor's comment: he said it looked "a bit like Pepto-Bismol." Needless to say, I felt that all my time, all my effort, had been wasted. My grade on the painting was a C. I was more disappointed by my wasted time than my grade. When I talked with my professor after class, I explained that I had worked very hard on the painting because of the time I spent on it. He responded, "So, if Picasso spends twenty hours on a piece, or ten minutes on a piece, does it matter? Or is it still a Picasso?"

I recall my professor's comment every time my colleagues debate that age-old question about teaching writing: Is writing an art, and therefore something that cannot really be taught? If so, what is an English teacher supposed to do?

I think writing can be viewed as art, but I do not believe this contradicts the idea that writing can be taught. Picasso was a gifted artist, no doubt, but he created brilliant works of art through years of practice and effort. The more he practiced, the more quickly he was able to produce some of his art pieces. In short, Picasso *wasted* very little time. I wasted a large portion of my time creating the first piece for my visual arts course, but as the semester progressed, I learned how to use my time more effectively. I never produced brilliant art, but, as in my experiences with dance, I did improve—in part because of practice, and also due to clear expectations from my instructor that allowed me to focus my effort. I moved from Cs to Bs, and toward the end of the semester, I even earned one A.

I bring up this example about grading art because I have heard so many teachers say over the years that writing, like art, is subjective, so how can we legitimately grade it? Some experts in the field of writing discourage grades altogether. Many tensions can arise when we have to grade writing, and I think we have to understand that even if grading writing is not best practice, we cannot just label grades as a "bad idea." Thousands of teachers must assign grades frequently in their writing classrooms. And if writing is in any way an art, then one important factor to consider is how to incorporate effort into our grading systems.

Grades and Effort

Okay. So hear me out. Effort should most definitely be graded. I think this because someone could spend hours and hours on one particular subject, and it turned out pretty formulaic. If the teacher does not like it though, that puts hours of work in the trash. No one would like that. If they get a bad grade, it would most likely begin a battleground between the parents and the teacher. To save time and appreciate hard work, effort should be in the grading rubric.

—Jane, Grade 7

This comment from seventh grader Jane, written on her classroom blog, provides a powerful charge to all of us: if a lot of effort is expended on creating something, then it is important to recognize this effort and to include it in our evaluation of student work. And if Jane is right—that effort unrewarded feels like "hours of work in the trash"—then we have to make sure our students' efforts are well spent. We need to monitor their progress during all parts of the writing process so that they do not find themselves frustrated with a low grade.

So how do we help students put forth meaningful effort, and then, how do we translate this into grades?

One of the problems with grading systems lies in how we tend to associate any piece of writing with a test. When teachers ask me to read work students have produced, they are almost apologetic if they feel they have helped a student with a piece. When I notice something good in a first-grade piece—for example, use of a strong verb—I often have teachers tell me, "Oh, but I helped with that" or "That word was on the word wall." This implies that, if a student received help, that student cannot be considered successful. I would maintain that we are holding our students to completely unrealistic standards if we cannot guide our writers.

If students' grades or proficiency ratings are lowered when we help them develop ideas, write, and revise, then something is wrong with the system. This may seem controversial when so many report cards ask students to perform tasks independently. In fact, a grade of A is often defined by the student's level of independence. But if a student is able to independently improve a piece of writing after a suggestion from a teacher, peer, or parent, then is this student not still independent?

Let's look at this idea of independence a little bit more carefully as we consider grades and effort.

Can we honor practice and effort when we grade, even if students are not quite meeting the standards? In other words, should I have received an A for Effort at the Martha Graham School or in my painting class even though I was, and will eternally be, the most beginning student in these venues? If we factor effort into grades, what about standards?

The reverse of this question must be considered as well, I suppose: if we do *not* consider effort when we grade, will we discourage students who are trying?

Clarity First

Clarity about the grading process is important if we want to help students become better writers. If I take home 120 papers over the weekend and I am surprised at the lack of quality, then I need to ask myself a difficult question: Was I clear about my expectations, and did I scaffold for students during their drafting and practice stages so they had a chance to succeed? I think any time we assess writing, we are assessing not only our students' progress but our own teaching.

If we plan our instruction so we know how students are doing along the way, everyone will have maximum opportunity for success. I do not believe this is antithetical to what happens in the "real world" of writing. Writers work with content editors during all parts of the writing process. Even Stephen King, author of more than fifty best-selling books, thanks his editor in his acknowledgments for helping him craft his ideas into books people will buy, often by asking him to delete unnecessary passages.

If a final copy is to be graded fairly, then, we must provide the opportunity for everyone to do well before he or she actually hands it in. I am not suggesting more grading here—in fact, I think that the time for actual grading can be cut down if we carefully plan out the cycle of when writing is actually turned in for a grade.

Try Not to Jump to Conclusions

As a teacher of writing, I often remind myself of Milo in *The Phantom Tollbooth*, whose adventures include a trip to the Island of Conclusions. Milo jumps to conclusions (literally) when he makes a decision without thinking. Milo wonders what happened, and Canby appears, ready to explain:

> *It's really quite simple: every time you decide something without having a good reason, you jump to Conclusions whether you like it or not. It's such an easy trip to make that I've been here hundreds of times. (Juster 1961, 168)*

As a teacher of writing, I have often made the same mistake. When I pick up a set of student papers and I choose to go error hunting, I jump to the conclusion that students need to work solely on mechanics in order to become better writers. But the truth about writing is much more complicated. Students often know the rules of writing, but they do not always apply them. If you doubt this, try showing your students a piece of your own writing, and include a few well-placed errors. If your students are like mine, they will immediately point out your mistakes. They do know a lot about writing, grammar, and mechanics, but they do not always demonstrate this by turning in self-edited pieces. When we refuse to jump to conclusions about student writing and slow down to gather a bit of data, we can support our student writers more effectively.

Allison Robertson noticed many of her second-grade students did not accurately place punctuation in their pieces, so she asked me to come in so we could develop a lesson together. When I looked at student writing samples, I noticed that the lack of punctuation was causing meaning to break down in many pieces, particularly the longer ones. We could have decided that these second graders just did not know anything about punctuation, and if we were in a particularly vengeful mood, we could have blamed the first-grade teachers even though we knew these students had been writing since kindergarten. But we did not take the Milo route of jumping to conclusions—instead, we slowed down and decided to gather more information. Our instructional move was context based: we decided to find out if students could identify the names and purposes of various punctuation marks in two sentences excerpted from a familiar picture book. I wrote the sentences on chart paper, we all read the text together fluently, and then I asked the students to identify the punctuation marks and why they were there.

It was clear within a few minutes that students did have a basic understanding of punctuation. They knew the difference between a question mark and a period, and they also knew commas were used to separate items in a list. We were then ready to see if they could use punctuation in their own writing.

Of course, some students in Allison's class were more successful in finding the places for their own punctuation than others. But since we realized they *knew* about punctuation, we could focus our teaching points on *application*. Students need plenty of time to practice showing what they know—and here again is where coaching metaphors can help us a bit. Good coaches expect and allow for plenty of practice time before the game, but as teachers of writing I wonder if we do allow enough time for our students to practice. After they demonstrate their understanding, we must realize that putting this knowledge to use is complex, because writing is such a creative task. In math, for example, 2 + 2 is always 4, but in writing, where to place a period is much more complicated than it first seems, because each student creates unique sentences. The nature of writing as a creative act is what challenged Allison's students as they edited their own work. Evaluation stops the learning process, so the key is to monitor progress as students practice and improve.

Progress Toward a Standard

So what do we do when we have a student who is completing all class work, demonstrates a general understanding of the material, listens in class, and revises, but still does not meet the requirements of the standards found in a rubric? When we think of Allison's class, mentioned previously, how do we monitor progress of students who are still having difficulty punctuating their own writing but who can identify the purposes of punctuation in other texts?

What if a student continually receives a score of unsatisfactory or partially proficient on a rubric? Even if the language is changed to "developing" or "you're not there yet!" most kids know what we mean by these euphemisms. We mean they are not meeting the requirements of the standards and, therefore, are not meeting expectations.

I have worked with students who fit this profile. One student who comes to mind was in my fifth-grade class. His writing was labeled "unsatisfactory" according to his fourth-grade report card, and during his first few days with me, he barely wrote more than a sentence. I think it is important to talk about labels such as "unsatisfactory" when we think about assessment and standards. Labels can be damaging because they can lower our expectations of student achievement. If I receive my class list and immediately focus on the low scores or proficiency ratings, I might lower my expectations. This is dangerous, because I believe students rise to what we expect of them.

Assessment data can be used to meet the needs of specific students, but nothing should take the place of a fresh start and an opportunity for a student to make great gains. I once had a principal who encouraged us to pore over data so that we could really know our students as well as a doctor knows his or her patients, but I am not so sure the doctor/patient metaphor works in all cases. While we can use data to guide some of our decisions, we can also ask students to show us what they can do and go from there, especially in regard to writing. If the teachers at the Martha Graham School had used any data to determine what to do with me before I entered the school's summer workshop, they may not have let me in! And because they had high expectations of everyone, we all grew.

The student who was labeled "unsatisfactory" at the end of fourth grade did not write much for the first few weeks of fifth grade. I could have shown him his rubric scores, which were all in the lowest ranges based on a holistic score of 4. On traits-based rubrics, he still scored in the 1 and 2 range when all the traits were scored separately. However, I chose not to share these scores with him at the time because I knew they would defeat any confidence he was starting to build. Instead, I chose to tell him what he was doing well and to pinpoint one thing he could work on. For the first two months of school, the only thing I focused on was getting him to write *more*. I praised him for what he did write—"This makes sense" I would say, or I would comment on the content specifically—"I love dogs too; tell me more"—and I would just make sure he added meaningful details.

When he wasn't sure what to write, I would talk with him and then offer to write one sentence of what he just shared if he would write the next. I firmly believed that with enough gentle coaching he would eventually write, and he did.

The first report card period came twelve weeks into school. He had made great progress, but his scores were not at grade level. I chose not to give him the "unsatisfactory" label because I had proof that he had made progress and was beginning to internalize some of the qualities of a writer.

I believe that we can justify passing grades if students are making progress *toward* a standard—we do not have to just wait until they get there. Here was a student who was barely producing a sentence when he arrived, and by twelve weeks into school, he was adding two to four details to each of his pieces independently. By January he was writing complete, two- to three-page pieces with minimal support.

I knew that if he kept up the trajectory—if he kept improving—he would eventually have a strong chance of becoming proficient. And he was proficient according to fifth-grade standards by the end of the year.

My belief is that writing *can* be taught. Did this student I am describing ever love to write? Not particularly. But I knew I could teach him *how* to write with meaning and clarity if he would trust me and if I could start to help him see himself as a writer. I was not just "giving" him a grade and a standards-based satisfactory rating as a gift for seat time, but for the improvement he made. I monitored his progress every day to make sure his efforts paid off, and over time, he did produce writing that met my projection from early in the year. He just needed a bit more time.

What Exactly Does Independence Mean?

I am going to return to kindergarten for a moment here as we think about the level of independence we require of students, and then I am going to skip all the way to graduate school.

When I visit kindergarten classrooms, I am impressed with how teachers are aware of each of their learners, and how they seem to effortlessly guide their charges in just the right way to move them to more independent thinking and learning. The words *kindergarten* and *effortless* should never appear in the same sentence, by the way, but I am just being honest when I tell you that so many of the kindergarten teachers I have the honor of working with seem to know how to meet the needs of individual students.

Bea Arteaga is one such teacher. Whenever I visit her during writing workshop, students know what to do. And they also know who and what to ask when they need support. Some students are writing sentences early in the year, while others are barely able to label their pictures with initial consonant sounds. But as Bea moves through the room, she provides the right type of assistance to each student. Some are ready to say words slowly and listen for beginning, middle, and ending sounds, whereas others are ready only for the initial sound. She does not do any of the work for them, but she does help them.

I am going to jump ahead to my experiences in graduate school now. When I took literary criticism with Brad Mudge at the University of Colorado at Denver, I struggled reading Derrida. Since I had sixteen years of education under my belt, should Brad have left me to my own devices, assuming I was an "independent learner"? I am glad to say he helped me, and the rest of the "struggling readers" in the class, to understand how to read incredibly dense literary analysis. And my professor Margaret Whitt at the University of Denver took me aside during graduate school and helped me to identify the places in my writing where I used passive voice. I thank her to this day.

Should Brad and Margaret have docked my grades because I did not independently, without help, do everything that was asked? Should Bea think of her students as struggling writers because they need various kinds of support?

We need to be very careful about how we define this need for independence, because it can cause very good teachers to use practices that are not benefiting student learning. If students need support, we should provide it. We need to balance our support by expecting a level of independence so students do not rely completely on us, but we should be there as they write so that they can improve.

We need to remember that state tests, SATs, and ACTs, though very high-stakes, are really just events. And the best way to prepare students to be successful on these tests is not to create multiple situations where they get no support so we can claim to be getting them ready for the test. Instead, we need to provide them with every opportunity to become more confident learners by scaffolding our instruction along the way.

Talking with Students About Grades

My ideas about how effort can be incorporated into grading began with a student comment on a classroom blog. I also learned a lot about successful grading practices when I asked students at various levels what they thought about grades. When teachers discuss grades, they typically talk about how overwhelming it is to keep up with the paper load. Students, however, mention fairness. I have yet to meet a student who disagreed with a grade as long as it was "fair."

Jesse is one such student. I met him when he was in sixth grade, and he told me about his experiences with writing the year before. He felt that his fifth-grade teacher did not like his work and was therefore unfair. He told me about a long story he wrote in his class that his teacher didn't like. "She thought it was too boyish," he told me. "I told a story with weapons and stuff." His biggest complaint was about the effort he put into this story—he reminded me of seventh grader Jane's comments, who said that wasted effort is like "hours of work in the trash."

When he was in sixth grade, Jesse shared his portfolio with me. That year, he felt that the grades were fair. He was worried at first about having Mrs. Widmann for a teacher because he heard she was "hard," but he thrived in her class. I asked him to talk to me about his writing using pieces from his writer's notebook and his portfolio.

He showed me pieces from earlier in the year that he thought were not very good. "They're too short, and I don't use any figurative language in them. I'm working on figurative language this year." I asked Jesse to show me a piece he was proud of, and he chose a piece full of details and imagery. His grade on this single piece was 15/20, or a C. On this particular piece, Mrs. Widmann was grading only for mechanics, and his work had not met her very high standards. But he knew that he could revise and resubmit this piece later in the term as proof that he was meeting the content standards in her class. He didn't mind the C at all because he knew that she would be fair when it came time to prove what he knew.

When I asked Jesse what he liked about Mrs. Widmann's class, he immediately mentioned her use of "weird prompts." He gave an example: "We had to write one day about if we were more like a potato or a waterfall. I thought that was pretty funny—I chose a potato because my brothers pick on me all the time and I feel like a mashed potato."

I was curious about the prompt idea, so I asked him why he liked the prompts. He said, "Because there is no right answer. We just get to write." But Jesse also knows that if he is proud of his prompt-writing exercises, he can bring them to Mrs. Widmann as evidence of meeting her standards to improve his grades.

Let's think about what Pam Widmann is doing in her classroom practice for a few minutes. When she grades, she often focuses on a single part of the writing process. She provides students with many opportunities to write: each student in her class keeps a writer's notebook for quick-write (Jesse's "weird prompt") exercises, and each student also keeps a portfolio of drafts and final copies that are assigned as each term progresses. Pam labels her grades by standard. As the end of a grading term nears, she quickly determines if students need work in a particular area of writing, and she can also ask students to provide her with examples of how well they are writing before she finalizes grades.

Pam's method of grading saves time because she often grades pieces on only one or two standards, and she also avoids the need to average. In other words, if she looks at Jesse's grades and notes that he has not met a proficiency level in figurative language, she can ask him to produce a piece that demonstrates his growth in this area. He can use an existing piece, revise a piece, or craft a new one—but he knows exactly what is expected of him. He has a chance to demonstrate what he has learned and how he has grown. In a standards-based grading system, it is unnecessary to grade everything and average assignments, because students need to demonstrate that they have met the standard, not that they have maintained a 90 percent average over time.

I asked another student in Pam's class, Megan, about her grades and motivation. She was proud of how far her writing had come since being in the class, and I asked her if she found grades motivating or not.

"What if you get a grade that you are disappointed about? What do you do?" I asked.

Megan said that grades made her want to improve, and that Pam's comments and her clear rubrics (developed with students' input, as described in Chapter 3) helped. "Grades motivate me to do better," she told me.

Until I asked her specifically about grades, however, Megan only talked about her writing, her goals, and her pride in improving. She was willing to talk about grades when cued, but that was not her focus when we sat down to look at her portfolio.

Many teachers tell me they are frustrated by assigning a single score to a process as complex as writing, but my discussions with students convince me there are ways to help them focus on improving their work rather than on getting higher grades. I believe one key to deemphasizing grades is in monitoring the talk in the classroom: If the talk is consistently about writing and the qualities of strong writing, then our message to students is about quality, not grades. If I choose to repeatedly remind my students how to raise a grade instead of how to improve the writing, then I am asking them to work for the grade and not for the quality.

Jesse and Megan are cases in point here: they only mentioned grades when I specifically brought them up, and Jesse even showed me the piece he received a low score on as his best work because he assumed we were there to talk about the quality of writing.

When students talked to me about "fair" grading practices, these traits were commonly mentioned:

- Clear expectations
- The opportunity to get support prior to a final assignment's being due
- An opportunity to demonstrate learning as the grading term ends—not so much a chance to "redo" a piece in order to receive a higher grade, but an opportunity to show what you have learned

The last descriptor places the emphasis on grades where I think it should be: on growth and progress. And if we think back to Jane's comment, what we are really providing is an opportunity for students to show how their efforts have paid off.

I visited Jan DiSanti's fourth-grade classroom to discuss the same issues about grades. In my district, fourth grade is the first level when students receive actual letter grades on their report cards. This first year of grades can be difficult for some students because they might focus more on their grades than on their learning. But, as in Pam Widmann's sixth-grade class, I found that strong teaching practices defuse anxiety about grades.

Tiana mentioned that if she received a bad grade, she would first look at some of her own writing to see if she could do a better job. "First I would compare it with one of my pieces I did a good job on, then I would see how I went down. Another idea is I would think of more ways to make my writing better. If that didn't work, I would go to Ms. DiSanti for more support."

Sade, Tiana's friend, sat in on this discussion and agreed that the first place she would look for support was her own writing. When I asked them if they had ever been discouraged about writing, they said they had, but that the best way to move on and to get support was by talking to other students in the room. Their sources of support were clear to these students: their own writing, the help of their teacher, and discussions with peers and family members. These students were able to name specific sources of support independently, which means they had internalized their own writing processes. The time that Jan has spent helping her students understand how they can improve their own writing has paid off, because as these students encounter difficulty, they will be able to seek the support they need. I have visited Jan's classroom many times, and one of her many strengths is her ability to help students *own* their learning. She has very high expectations, and she differentiates with ease because her students know what they need to be successful.

Franny, another student in Jan's class, discussed the changes in her grades during the year. In the first grading period, Franny received a C. By the second term, she had improved and received a B.

"What did you do to improve your grade? What made the difference for you?" I asked.

"I was encouraged by teachers and I was more focused. They encouraged me to not play around with my friends and to work harder," Franny replied.

"So were other things in class getting in the way of your learning? Did it discourage you when your teachers pointed this out?"

"No."

"What did you improve in your writing?"

"More details. Sometimes my writing doesn't make sense because I didn't include enough details. My friends would tell me that my writing didn't make sense because I didn't have details."

"Are there certain students in class who help you with your writing?"

"Yes. I go to Hailey because she is an extraordinary writer. And she doesn't lie. She will tell me the truth about my writing and it really helps me."

Franny is reiterating what I heard from other students. Her effort, when focused, paid off. And it is interesting to hear this student, all of ten years old, continually focus on how much her writing has improved. Even though she is graded because she is in a school system, she never mentioned grades on her own—she kept talking about how she was hoping to improve her writing, and she knew where she could get support in order for this to happen.

After several interviews, I talked with Jan's whole class about grades and how to make sure grades were fair. They felt that as long as they could go back and try again, they didn't mind grades, even if they were low. I assumed they were talking about a chance to revise.

"So you mean that as long as you have a chance to revise a piece for a better grade, the grades don't bother you?"

"Or, we could just start a new piece to show how we are getting better," said Franny.

"You don't want to revise the old one?"

"No, not always."

I asked students to raise their hands if they would rather start a new piece to show how they were improving as opposed to revising an old piece.

All of the students voted for starting a new piece. This is not a scientific survey, but it was interesting information for Jan and I to discover. We talked about the possibility of building in enough time before the end of each grading period for students to start new pieces that demonstrated their best work. They liked this idea.

Again, it is not just important to know your students as writers—it is essential. I share these examples as models for beginning a dialogue with students about fair grading practices. I am sure that Pam's and Jan's students next year may have some different ideas, but I am also certain their students will have a voice. Their teachers will listen to them because they know that assessment is an important topic to discuss, especially when the proper use of assessment can lead to more informed teaching and better writing. When students are allowed to help define what is fair and to collaborate with teachers as assessment routines are defined and carried out, they are more likely to work hard to become strong writers.

Summing Up: A Balanced Approach to Teaching

When I think about grades now, after spending a lot of time talking with students and teachers and reflecting on the many ways I have tried to grade student work, I have come to the conclusion that we must have balance. Part of me wishes we could just get rid of grades altogether—but then, when I talked with students, I realized they only became stressed about grades when they felt the grading practices themselves were unfair.

Here is a summary of tips from this chapter that will help you achieve a balance as you consider your own grading practices:

- Make sure that effort is honored in some way in your classroom. If students are working hard toward meeting your standards, then their efforts should pay off by raising the quality of their writing.

- Clarify the meaning of "independence" as you consider your grading practices, and be cautious about equating tests with the only "real" independent indicator of student success.

- Separate student knowledge and application. Do not assume students do not understand the qualities of good writing just because they do not always produce it. First, determine if it is a problem of knowledge or application.

- Monitor student progress while you read and grade student work. Be cautious about sharing low rubric scores or grades with students if they do not allow these students to see how they have grown. Try to find ways to frequently show students, concretely, how they are growing as writers.

• Discuss grades with students as a way to demonstrate how they are growing rather than making them feel "stuck." Be cautious about grades that reflect incomplete homework or assignments rather than grades that reflect student achievement. The more closely grades track student progress toward a standard, the less surprising grades will be to students.

• Build in time before the end of each grading period for students to improve as writers. Do not wait until a few days before the end of a grading term to surprise yourself, your students, and parents about low grades that could have been improved.

• Allow students opportunities to demonstrate their growth as writers. Let them decide if they are going to revise an existing piece or start a new one.

6

6

Keeping Records, Keeping Track

I belonged to a book discussion group for fifteen years. I enjoyed this opportunity to talk about books with other adults, even when the "teacher" in me wanted to guide the discussion, always ready with a thought-provoking question.

The only problem for me with this monthly meeting was the night we met: Sunday. Sunday nights are notoriously stress-inducing for teachers. We have a hard time focusing on anything except the papers we have to grade, and as soon as we tell ourselves we must grade, and keep up on our grading, we set ourselves up for being solely responsible for an enormous task: evaluating dozens, or hundreds, of student writing samples each week.

As I have suggested throughout this book, assessment must encompass so much more than grading. We should rewind that Sunday night scene of the teacher on the couch surrounded by papers and think about why we are reading student work in the first place. If we do not move beyond the idea of grading every time we read student work, then we may never break out of the assign-and-grade cycle that does not result in stronger student writing.

Since we ask students to read for authentic purposes, why can't we? What if we changed our thinking about *why* we read student work?

A few years ago, I visited a second-grade classroom and I heard the teacher cueing her students to share what they noticed about a piece of writing a boy had shared. She said, "What do you admire about John's writing?"

Admire.

What a verb. What if we read student work to *admire* what students are doing well? Can you imagine telling your Sunday night book club you have to leave a bit early because you have to go home and *admire*, instead of *grade*, student work? They might think it is time for you to retire, but I can tell you that when I read with the purpose of finding student strengths, there are many benefits: I do not lose energy by becoming an "error hunter," I can use my positive comments about student work to build a writing community through conferences and public acknowledgment of strong student writing samples, and I can even begin marking student progress toward a standard by noticing strengths first.

So how can I read student work for various purposes and still keep in mind all of the planning and assessing I need to do? In the next part of the book, I will offer suggestions in two parts—one focused on reading a single piece of student writing, and one focused on reading multiple pieces.

Reading One Piece of Student Work

Anne Finseth's third graders created picture books as a final project for their personal narrative study. One of Anne's students, Veronica, wrote a piece about getting a hamster for her birthday (see Figure 6.1).

If I think of only *grading* Veronica's work, I might become overwhelmed by too many considerations, and I might also miss opportunities for helping Veronica become a stronger writer. If I get out my red pen, I might only notice her misspelling of *sparkly* as "sparkily" and *polka dots* as "pokadots." I might be concerned about the tense changes or even wonder how this piece will eventually lead to a story about a pet. When I move to *grade* a piece first, I am focused on only one purpose and I therefore might limit my students' opportunities for growth.

Figure 6.1
Veronica's final project

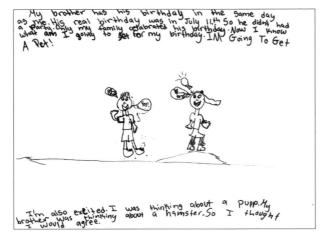

Figure 6.1 (continued)

But FIRST my family and I had to check animal we wanted. My mom said no to the puppy. Cause she didn't want a puppy. Because she thought are garden was to small.

My brother wanted to get a hamster because my cousin Gracie had a hamster and its name was Max. And I thought it was cool. First we had to go to the mall and check which pet we wanted.

When we went to the mall I saw puppies and hamsters and tons of birds. Then we actually didn't get nothing there so we went to Pet Co. So I had to think realy hard. It was also hard to picks the pet that I wanted. I saw hamsters, a rabbit, snakes, lizards, fishes, and birds and cats. I realy took my time.

Figure 6.1 (continued)

When we went to PetCo I saw this cat. I thought it was a nice cat but no it was a mean cat. It was a mean cat because when you tap on the plastic window it sticks out its paws at you. Like if it was going to scrach you.

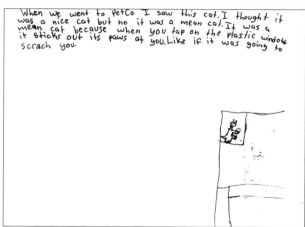

And my mom wanted a bird and also my dad wanted a bird but we didnt want to get a bird. So then I wanted a hamster for my birthday. And it was Saturday I was super excited.Cause remember my birthday is on Sunday.

Figure 6.1 (continued)

Finally it was my birthday we went to the Zoo it was pretty fun. Then we went to Pet Co I was looking at the hamsters cause I realy wanted a hamster and the hamsters were asleep All of them were black and white. I think I know which hamster I will get. It was in the left side of a animal shelf.

Then I had to ask a women so I could get my pet. Suddenly a man came and telled us "What do you need". Then I said "could I have a hamster" then the man opened the cage.

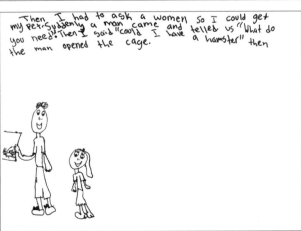

Figure 6.1 (continued)

He gave me the hamster and then he went to get a box then I put the hamster in there.

The box had little holes in there so the hamster could breath and we had to buy all the sulplice. I named him Shadow. Now were going home.

When I think of what to *admire* about Veronica's piece, however, I can do so much more than when I think of grading or evaluating. I can admire how effectively Veronica uses just the right amount of description when she discusses the outfit her mother bought her. I can admire the way she moves the narrative through time, providing details about going to the pet store, the zoo, and then again to the pet store to get the hamster she has been waiting for.

When I choose something to admire first, I not only stifle the editor in me but also find ideas for conferences. The first rule of thumb when conferring with students is to begin with the positive, so noticing something Veronica has done well serves two purposes: I can record her strengths for assessment purposes, and I can also develop a conversation starter for our conference.

Since I never hear teachers complain about having too much planning time, I try to find ways to incorporate planning into any reading of student work. I am looking for strengths in Veronica's piece anyway, so why not keep an eye out for a writing craft technique she has used that can become a model for the rest of the class? When I do this, I am moving from reading one paper that can guide my thinking about one student to finding something I can teach to my whole class. For example, I have never visited a third-grade classroom where the students would not benefit from a discussion about the right amount of description. I call this the "Goldilocks theory" of description: we want just the right amount of descriptive writing. Not too much, not too little, but just right. Since Veronica has provided just a few descriptive adjectives in the section about the clothes her mother bought her, I can use her text as a model for the whole class. I can quickly share an excerpted page from her piece, and I can ask students to think about the right amount of descriptive language when they write their own pieces.

So in this one instructional move—reading to admire—I have accomplished three things:

1. I have read and recorded Veronica's individual strengths.
2. I have selected possible topics to begin a conference.
3. I have found possibilities for using student work as a model during a mini-lesson.

I list these separately to demonstrate *how* I am assessing Veronica as a writer: instead of becoming the editor who looks only for errors, I am first looking for strengths. I am assessing in a positive way, rather than in a way that will only allow me to focus on what is wrong.

Once I have admired Veronica's piece, I can move on to looking for possible learning targets. Here, it is essential to know as much about the student as possible. Most students can only handle one or two suggestions for improvement at a time, and we must make sure we base our decisions on what students already know and are able to do. I have noted that Veronica's strengths include specific supporting details, a strong sense of voice in both pictures and text, and some strong descriptive words. One default technique I use when choosing a learning target is to capitalize on the students' strengths. For example, in this piece, Veronica describes her clothes at the beginning, but she does not describe the hamster later in the piece. Since she has already demonstrated an ability to describe, and I know I will mention this when I talk with her, I can always ask her to use descriptive writing skills on the page when she buys her hamster. I am asking her to replicate a craft she has already used. Another possibility is to consider other writing crafts or skills that I want this student to incorporate in this piece—but again, knowing the student is absolutely necessary. For example, I may decide Veronica can work on a lead that sets the reader up to want to know more about her hamster. Or I may ask her to examine sentence beginnings and lengths. If I have been working in class on subject-verb agreement and tense changes, then I may want to ask Veronica about pages where she changes her verb tenses. None of these are right or wrong instructional moves, but my decisions should be made so that Veronica feels empowered. I also must consider efficiency. Since most of us do not have the luxury of teaching an individual student brand-new material for fifteen- or twenty-minute stretches, I will need to select a learning target Veronica can act upon in a short time frame.

In addition to the learning target, I must also consider how Veronica will demonstrate how she grows after our conference. For example, let's say that I notice when I read Veronica's picture book that she needs to think about balance: her piece is mainly about the hamster, but at times she moves on to other topics within the day and gives these ideas more attention than the hamster. My teaching point is about balance, but should I ask her to revise the piece she has already written or should I instead ask her to consider balance the next time she writes? I typically consider where we are in the writing process when I think about the "now" or "later" choice. I know that Veronica's piece is filled with energy and voice. I know she has produced a final copy that has been shared with her class and her family. Because of this, I probably won't ask her to go in and change this piece, but rather, I may have a discussion with her during the planning stages the next time she writes. I might talk with her about her ideas and help her to figure out where to place the emphasis in her writing.

I must always compare Veronica to herself as I make these decisions about what to teach her. In other words, I am not going to leave Veronica with the impression she did something wrong. I want to emphasize what is right first and then find teaching points that can make her a stronger, more confident writer.

Reading Multiple Papers

I have demonstrated how we can help our entire class by reading just one piece of student work, but more often, we must read an entire set of papers to actually determine how to inform our instruction. Even when faced with a stack of papers, though, there are ways to be efficient.

Let me give an example. I have a stack of twenty-four pieces of fifth-grade student work in front of me, and I begin reading the first piece. I am reading intentionally with the purpose of finding a strength in each student's writing. While I read, I have both a rubric and a record sheet next to me. On the record sheet, I have included room for recording possible mini-lesson topics based on what I learn while reading student work (see Figure 6.2; also in appendix).

Figure 6.2

WRITING RECORD SHEET

Date _____   Genre_____

Name	Main Idea	Specific Details	Multiple Details	Organization	Word Choice	Conventions

NUMBER CODES

4 = clearly meets standard
3 = strengths outweigh weaknesses
2 = weaknesses outweigh strengths
1 = no evidence of meeting standard

LETTER CODES

S = strength L = learning target
M = student model for mini-lesson
Mini-lesson needs:

When I read Brian's paper (Figure 6.3), the first in my stack, I notice he has a clear main idea (he hates broccoli), but needs more supporting details. I am using the rubric below the chart to help me score this piece, so I record a 4 for main idea and a 2 for supporting details. However, I do notice that the details he has are actually clear and specific, so I note a conference starter on my record sheet with an *S*. I also add Brian's piece to my list of possible mini-lessons below the table on the record sheet and note that his work can promote the use of specific details.

Figure 6.3
Brian's piece

Name **brian**

Write about a food you do not like to eat.

One food that I hate
eating is is anything with
brocli. I hate brocil because
and it take forever to chew
I think brocli taste worse
then eating oines. I Reather
eat PaPer insted of brocli.
brocli taste horbile

When I move on to Owen's piece (Figure 6.4), I immediately notice that, according to the rubric language, his use of supporting details puts his piece in the 4 category. I note below the table that I can use this piece as an example of the use of multiple supporting details in a mini-lesson. Owen needs to work on his organization and his use of conventions, so I note this by recording a 2 in each of these categories on the record sheet.

Figure 6.4
Owen's piece

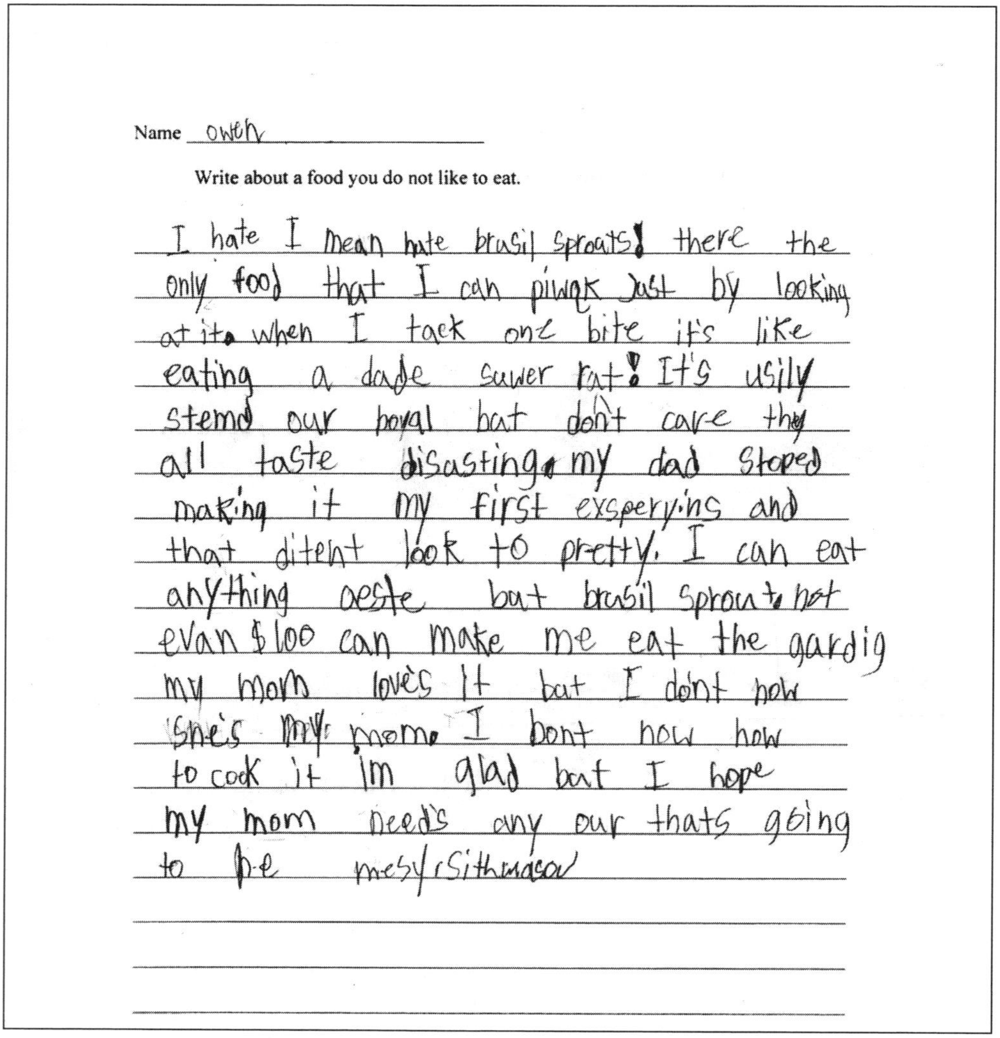

Name ___owen_____

Write about a food you do not like to eat.

I hate I mean hate brusil sproats! there the only food that I can piwak just by looking at it. when I tack one bite it's like eating a dade suwer rat! It's usily stemd our boyal but don't care they all taste disasting. my dad stoped making it my first exsperyins and that ditent look to pretty. I can eat anything oeste but brusil sprouts not evan $100 can make me eat the gardig my mom loves it but I don't how she's my mom. I dont how how to cook it im glad but I hope my mom needs any our thats going to be mesyrsithuagow

Much like how I looked at Veronica's piece earlier, I can accomplish multiple tasks by reading this group of fifth graders' pieces:

1. I have recorded student strengths so that I can keep track of how I might want to begin a conference or a brief discussion with each student about a strength

2. I have recorded possibilities for teaching points (anything less than a 4) for each student.

3. I have recorded possibilities for mini-lessons based on students' strengths. I know that I can find professional mentor texts very easily to compare the students' work to. To begin each mini-lesson, I can briefly read an excerpt from a student piece and an excerpt from the corresponding professional piece. Then I can describe the importance of the writing craft technique.

While this may sound time consuming, I recorded the information on the completed record sheet (see Figure 6.5) in about forty minutes. This record will be useful to me for several days as students continue working and as I decide on what mini-lessons will benefit the class.

Figure 6.5
Completed Writing Record Sheet

Fifth Grade Writing Record Sheet

Date Dec. 10, 2008
Genre prompt practice

Name	Main Idea	Specific Details	Multiple Details	Organization	Word Choice	Conventions
Brian	4	4 MS	2 L	3	3	2
Owen	4	4 MS	4 ms	2 L	4	2
Alexis	4	4	4	4 ms	3	4 m
Tristin	4	4 S	4	3 L	4	3 m
Josselene	3	4 S	4	2 L	3	3
Josiah	4	4 S	4	2 L	3	2
Ashurtie	4 S	2 L	2	2	2	2
Chaday	3	3 S	2 L	3	3	3
Maciah	4 S	3	3	2 L	3	2
Taylor	4	3	2 L	2	3	3
Angelo	4	4 ms	3	2 L	3	3
Serhey	4	4 S	4	2 L	3	3
Sam	3 L	2	2	2	3 S	2
Helen	4	4 S	2 L	2	3	3
Max	4	2 L	3 S	2	3	2
Maria	4	4	4	4 ms	3 L	4
Ray	4	4	3	2 L	3	2
Arianna	4	4	4	3	3 L	3
Monique	4 S	2 L	2	2	2	2
Yasmine	4	3	2 L	3	3	2
Cynthia	4	4	4	4 S	3 L	4
Frank	4	4	4	3 L	4	3
Dante	4	4	3	3 L	3	3
CJ	4	4	2 L	2	3	2

Number codes
4 = clearly meets standard
3 = strengths outweigh weaknesses
2 = weaknesses outweigh strengths
1 = no evidence of meeting standard

Letter codes
S = strength   L = learning target
M = student model for mini-lesson
Mini-lesson needs:

When I look at the entire record sheet, I can now make some decisions about what my students need next. Because ten students have yet to demonstrate strengths in organization, and only three have clearly met this standard, it seems logical to use these three students' samples as models for how to organize a written piece. Most students have seemed to master specific details, while others are not as strong at including multiple details to support their intentions as writers. From reading this one set of papers, I have three samples of student writing that can serve as models for specific details, one for multiple details, and the three already mentioned for organization.

The learning targets (recorded with an *L* on the record sheet) indicate my future work with individual students. Since ten students have targets for organization, this will be the basis of my next mini-lesson. Hopefully, many, if not all, of these students will improve their writing on their own after the mini-lesson. I have other students with learning targets for specific details, multiple details, and word choice, so as I walk around the room and confer with students I can begin to talk with individuals about these targets. I have also indicated each student's individual strengths (noted with an *S*) so that I can offer praise at the beginning of each conference.

There are times when we read student work and notice that all students need the same teaching point, and we may not have any student models to use for a mini-lesson. For example, what would have happened if I read all of the pieces from this fifth-grade class and noticed the need for organization, but no students had actually written a completely organized piece? If this happens, I have a few options:

1. I can create a piece of my own writing and then tell the students I have struggled with the same thing they are struggling with. I can cue them to help me make my piece more organized, for example, if I noticed they were struggling in this area. After we work on my piece, they can work on their own in the same manner.

2. I can find a professional piece of writing that exhibits the qualities missing in student work samples. Once we examine the strengths of the professional model, I can ask students to see if they can revise their own pieces demonstrating these strengths.

3. We can write a piece together as a class during the mini-lesson, and I can cue students to think carefully about the craft or skill I want them to focus on. For example, since I am concerned about organization in the student writing I just collected, I can ask students to help me create a piece of writing about a topic we have just studied in class or about an experience we have all had. When students provide examples of details we might include in our piece, I can first list the details and then talk about how to organize them.

Do Standards Limit Surprises?

There is an inherent problem with labeling a record sheet with specific standards: What if students do something unusual, and they actually write something not covered in the standards on my record sheet or rubric? What if they surprise me? This happens to me all the time—and when it does, I am so glad that I can remain surprised. In the group of fifth-grade student writing described in the last section, for example, my student Frank indicated that he would not allow green beans if he was in charge. Instead of writing this in a typical fashion, however, he wrote: "In the United States of Frank . . ." as a repeated line to specify what would and would not be allowed in regard to food in "his" country. Frank's unique voice shines here. Though I am not technically recording students' use of voice in this particular piece, I can certainly praise Frank during a conference, or I can share his piece with the class as an example of a unique style. My point here is that, although I have categorized my reading of student work on the record sheets in Figures 6.2 and 6.5, I keep myself open to the element of surprise because I first look to admire—to notice a strength. In the United States of Frank, I welcome pleasant surprises in student writing.

Summing Up

Obviously, we sometimes need to grade student work. But if we *only* grade or evaluate, we become the ones with all the answers, and we create an environment where it is nearly impossible to move beyond merely assigning and grading. The record-keeping systems suggested in this chapter are meant to support reading student work for various purposes and keeping track of this work.

So this Sunday night, read to *admire* student work and see what happens when you walk into your classroom Monday morning, excited to share what you noticed. You may not dread future Sundays as much as before, and your students may actually begin to believe in themselves as writers. And remember what staff developer and writer Carl Anderson shared at a conference I attended: *assess* comes from the Latin word meaning "to sit beside." When you look at student writing, you are not standing in a place of judgment. Rather, you are sitting beside your students, and they are helping you, guiding you, teaching you what to do next.

Appendix

Writing Checklist

CONTENT AND ORGANIZATION

____ I included important details in my writing.

____ My writing has a clear main idea.

____ My writing is organized and logical: the ideas fit together.

____ My writing has a clear purpose.

STYLE AND FLUENCY

____ I used awesome words: specific nouns, descriptive adjectives, and strong verbs.

____ I used just the right amount of similes, metaphors, sensory details, or imagery to help make a picture in the reader's mind.

____ Some of my sentences are long, and some of them are short. Not all of my sentences begin with the same word.

____ I checked my writing for errors in spelling, capitalization, and punctuation.

MY WRITING PROCESS

	What works for me	What doesn't work
Getting ready to write/Idea making		
Writing/Drafting		
Revising/Editing		
Goals		

MY WRITING PROGRESS

Name _____

CONTENT AND ORGANIZATION

My writing has a clear main idea.

1. _____   2. _____   3. _____

I included important details in my writing.

1. _____   2. _____   3. _____

My writing is organized and logical: the ideas fit together.

1. _____   2. _____   3. _____

MY WRITING PROGRESS (CONTINUED)

STYLE AND FLUENCY

I used awesome words:
- specific nouns
- descriptive adjectives
- and strong verbs

1. _____ 2. _____ 3. _____

I used just the right amount of
- similes,
- sensory details,
- or imagery to help make a picture in the reader's mind

1. _____ 2. _____ 3. _____

I wrote some long sentences, and some short sentences. Not all of my sentences begin with the same word.

1. _____ 2. _____ 3. _____

I have almost no errors in
- capitalization
- punctuation
- spelling

1. _____ 2. _____ 3. _____

WRITING RECORD SHEET

Date _____   Genre_____

Name	Main Idea	Specific Details	Multiple Details	Organization	Word Choice	Conventions

NUMBER CODES

4 = clearly meets standard
3 = strengths outweigh weaknesses
2 = weaknesses outweigh strengths
1 = no evidence of meeting standard

LETTER CODES

S = strength L = learning target
M = student model for mini-lesson
Mini-lesson needs:

Bibliography

Anderson, Carl. 200... ...tudent Writers. Portsmouth, NH:

Anderson, Jeff. 200... ...Style into Writer's Workshop. Portla...

———. 2007. Everyda... ...Writer's Workshop. Portla...

Bernabei, Gretchen, ...Voice Lessons in Persuasive Writin...

Black, Paul, Christi... ...am. 2004. "Working Inside ... ...om." Phi Delta Kappan 86 (1): 9–...

Colorado Departme...

Goldberg, Natalie. 1... ...: Rider.

Graves, Donald H., a... ...o Teach the Details of Craft. Portsmouth, NH:

Juster, Norton. 1961. ...dom House.

Leahy, Siobhan, Chri... ...Dylan Wiliam. 2005. "Classroom Assessment: Min... ...onal Leadership 63 (3): 19–24.

National Council of ... ...ional Reading Association (NCTE/IRA). 1996. Standards fo... ...rbana, IL: National Council of Teachers of English.

Popham, James W. 2... ...sment. Alexandria, VA: Association for Supervision and C... ...

Ray, Katie Wood. 1999. Wondrous Words: Writers and Writing in the Elementary Classroom. Urbana, IL: National Council of Teachers of English.

———. 2007. Study Driven: A Framework for Planning Units of Study in the Writing Workshop. Portsmouth, NH: Heinemann.

Ray, Katie Wood, with Lisa B. Cleaveland. 2004. About the Authors: Writing Workshop with Our Youngest Writers. Portsmouth, NH: Heinemann.

Rylant, Cynthia. 2000. In November. Orlando, FL: Harcourt.

———. 1991. Night in the Country. New York: Aladdin.

Spandel, Vicki. 2006. "In Defense of Rubrics." English Journal 96 (1): 19–22.

Wilson, Maja. 2006. Rethinking Rubrics in Writing Assessment. Portsmouth, NH: Heinemann.